D1516205

I have been witness to many scientific breakthroughs. Such marvels invariably were performed by people of great talent, vision and courage. Dr. Leo Frangipane approaches his world and his patients as our greatest scientists do — creating a breeding ground for unexpected healing.

Joseph A. Miller, Jr., Ph.D.
Senior Vice President and Chief Technical Officer, E.I.DuPont deNemours

Dr. Frangipane is a very valuable member of our surgical staff, recognized not only for his outstanding clinical capability but for his deep compassion and interpersonal skills.

Charles Sullivan
President/CEO, The Reading Hospital and Medical Center

Dr. Leo Frangipane is an empathetic physician whose deep compassion drives him to seek the healing of the entire person. His patients attest to the loving concern he has for them before, during, and after treatment. Touchstones and Wellsprings shares his experiences and his faith in the ministry of healing.

Rev. Msgr. James A. Treston
Dean, Berks County Catholic Clergy

This book skillfully bridges medicine and spiritualism. Dr. Leo's patients are encouraged to maximize their quality of life, to hope, to reach out, and to love.

Rabbi Alan Weitzman
Congregation Oheb Shalom
Co-author, *Making Sense Out of Sorrow*

The Survivor's Guide

Touchstones
and
Wellsprings

The Survivor's Guide

Touchstones and Wellsprings

by **Leo G. Frangipane, Jr., M.D.**

HARDY COMMUNICATIONS

Mohnton, Pennsylvania

Events and people discussed in this book are drawn from the life and practice of Dr. Leo Frangipane. Some actual names of people have been used with their permission. Other real scenarios use fictitious names so that a critical message can be shared without an invasion of privacy. The author is grateful to all who shared their storylines.

Cover and text illustrations compiled by Gretchen Hardy.

Library of Congress Catalog Card Number: 95-90414

ISBN 0-9647313-4-7

Reprinted 123456789

To my loving wife, Joyce . . .
for being the perfect template of positivism and
unconditional love. I couldn't have survived
without you!

To my special friend and role model, Dr. Bernie Siegel . . .
for his encouragement and support, but mostly for
teaching me what medicine was all about.

Wellsprings

"I don't believe it!" Luke said to Master Yoda.
Yoda replied, "That is why you fail."

Star Wars: The Empire Strikes Back

Contents

Touchstones

Name five good things that happened to you today.

Acknowledgments

"When are you going to write your book?!"

For years I've been encouraged to record my thoughts and experiences. I struggled with time constraints (The ubiquitous hope of *Some Day* kept my inertia satiated.) and self doubt (Were my experiences really as unique as I was being told?). Does the world really need another book on self healing and attitude adjustment?

I have many to thank for the help and encouragement that made this book possible.

To my patients, whose inspiration fill these pages, for their devotion during their times of trial.

To my friends, both living and with Our Lord, from our support group S.E.E.K., whose exceptional attitudes were my first inspiration.

To my peers, the large and silent majority of good physicians, who have learned the transition from curer to healer sometimes entails personal pain.

To my family, especially Joyce, Amy, Karen, Tina, Leo and Helen, for their loyalty, encouragement and example. You people are my best cheerleaders!

To my office staff, Sue, Wendy, Susie and Kelly, for their patience as they witnessed and upheld my daily struggle.

To my partner, Frank Carter, M.D., whose example and skill served as template.

To my friend, first editor, critic and publicist, Gretchen Hardy, who extracted from me, sometimes with great pain, the best I could offer, all the while tenderly nursing my ego.

To my friend, Joe Farrell, for countless hours of opinion and love.

Wellsprings

The greatest griefs are those we cause ourselves.

Sophocles

Foreword

I was different. I needed to accept and embrace this difference.

My medical practice thrived, yet I needed more. What? Many forces drove me to become a surgeon. Only one mattered. I loved people. Had I lost this guiding beacon? How could I get it back? Introspection was ever present, painful and yet necessary.

Friends of mine, Marcella and Kathy Boland, lost their husband and father to cancer. It was a difficult time. I had a small part in his ultimate healing through death.

One day a book, *Love, Medicine and Miracles* by Dr. Bernie Siegel, appeared on my desk. Written on the inside cover were the words, "Much of this could have been written by you." It was signed by the Bolands. Flattered and equally curious I read the book. The worldwide best seller of the mid '80s spoke of the pain, suffering, joy and ecstasy of being the physician. He told of one surgeon's attempt to solve his problem and become the very best privileged listener.

Mostly he talked about *healing* — not *curing* — as an attitude and not just this antibiotic or that dose of chemotherapy. Not so much the stainless steel of the surgeon's scalpel, but the grit and mettle of the sufferer's determination. Siegel related stories of great courage and grace among an exceptional group of patients labeled "terminal" or "incurable." He spoke of many defying the odds and ultimately winning their individual battles. Victory did not always come through living. Sometimes acceptance of death was the ultimate act of healing.

Years before I had read the chronicle *Man's Search for Meaning* by concentration camp survivor Viktor Frankl, whose experiences at Auschwitz spoke of horrible inhumanity. Frankl, a psychiatrist, spoke of survival. His most famous quotation is as meaningful today as it was fifty years ago. "To live is to suffer. To survive is to find meaning in the suffering."

Frankl understood what exceptional sufferers knew and what I was to discover. Ultimately, choice is up to the individual. No one, not those who love us or despise us, no stranger, family, lover, doctor or anyone — not even God Himself — can make us choose what we do not choose ourselves. Choice is the ultimate reason for survival.

The gift book spoke directly to me. On a whim, I called Dr. Bernie Siegel. Astonishingly, he returned my call! His secretary, Lucille Ranciato, a kindred Mediterranean, and I hit it off instantly over the phone; and I suspect it was her intercession that helped open the door. I begged to "hang out" with Bernie. He agreed. I went to Madison, Connecticut's Mercy Center (aptly named) to partake in a workshop. That week, nearly ten years ago, significantly altered and reaffirmed my path.

My experiences with Bernie and the hundred or so others with whom I shared that time turned my life around and were the skeleton of this book. Subsequent attention to my own patients eventually "fleshed out" the final text. They taught me the substance of "exceptional." Incurables with every conceivable disease — cancer, multiple sclerosis, AIDS, those HIV positive — and people with many kinds of neurological conditions, all spoke to me in a manner that was unique and distinctive. I finally listened with my heart and my head.

"Touchstones and Wellsprings" was not the original name chosen for this book. My good and dear friend, Gretchen Hardy, suggested this name after hearing me speak and digesting several chapters. *Touchstones* implies something fundamental, quintessential and true, the litmus test for purity. We both believed the contents and stories were true gold, not the kind fools pursue. Her thought about using *wellsprings* suggests that the source of the truths taught by my friends is in continual supply. All the listener need do is truly listen, not just hear the tales which contain the persistent source of essential truth.

This book is a sharing, a witnessing. It speaks of my interaction with those who strive to live each day as the miracle it genuinely is. The strength and enlightenment I was given, I impart to you. I truly hope you are inspired as many others have been as you journey on your path.

Wellsprings

And Jesus said, "The kingdom of heaven is within you."

Introduction

Grant Gordon was exceptional. His presence at our S.E.E.K. (Support and Encourage Exceptional Kinship) meetings was like coming home after a cold winter's day to a cup of cocoa by a cozy fireplace. Grant was a warm, positive, wonderful human being.

His courage was not the bravery found on battlefields but the heroism that comes with achieving true wisdom in the face of grave danger. Grant knew his lymphoma, currently under control, could rear its ugly head at any time; so he sought to touch as many people in his sphere of existence as he possibly could. Involvement in the local actors' guild provided a stage for his wonderful musical and acting talents. All those he touched experienced his caring and loving attitude. By his genuine involvement in S.E.E.K., he uplifted many lives with tales of trying to live on a daily basis.

Grant invited me to come to the county intermediate unit school where he was a teacher and counselor of physically and mentally disabled children, many teenagers. Grant was a talented pianist. God, how he could play! If the eyes are the windows to the soul, then Grant's fingers possessed vision. As they flew over the keys, his students, who often could not express their needs in other ways, danced with glee and clapped their hands. How privileged I was to witness his love in action.

Grant taught me that holding on too tightly to anything can squeeze out its life. Strangling and smothering was not his way. When a friend in our group died, it was Grant who made us realize how important it was to focus on the joy of having experienced that person in our lives. A funeral should be a time to celebrate life instead of memorializing death. Death, he insisted, was a healer, too.

Listen to what Dr. Bernie Siegel wrote about death:

A Great Teacher

Death,
What a great teacher you are.
Yet few of us elect to learn from you,
About life,
That is the essence of death's teaching,
Life.
Death is not an elective.
One day we all will take the class.
The wise students audit the class in early years
And find enlightenment.
They are prepared when graduation day comes.

———◆———

Before his death, Grant gave me a poem. Its source is unknown, but it speaks about the grace and peace of living that was Grant's way. Taken from us in his early manhood, Grant left scores of lives touched by his gentleness and love. Here is his gift to me:

Grant's Song: Nothing Is Forever

*After a while you learn the subtle difference
  between holding a hand and chaining a soul.
And you learn that love doesn't mean leaning and
  company doesn't mean security.
And you begin to learn that kisses aren't contracts
  and presents aren't promises.
And you begin to accept your defeats with your head
  up and your eyes ahead with the grace of a
  woman or a man not the grief of a child.
And you learn to build all your roads on today
  because tomorrow's ground is too uncertain for
  plans, and futures have a way of falling down in
  mid-flight.
After a while you learn that even sunshine burns
  if you ask too much.
So you plant your own garden and decorate your own
  soul instead of waiting for someone to bring you
  flowers.
And you learn that you really can endure, that you
  really are strong and you really do have worth.
And you learn
. . . and you learn
. . .with every good-bye
  you learn. . .*

I met this remarkable man at a time of restlessness in my life. Medicine's role was supposed to be more than just science. Some higher essence was needed to elevate my life's chosen profession. It seemed that the *art and heart* of the medicine I practiced had somehow slipped through my fingers like so many granules of sand. I had lost my compassion, empathy and fire. I had become a dispassionate, impersonal judge of diseases. A referee in scrubs. A surgeon who had somehow incised his own feelings.

Martin Buber, a Jewish theologian, said that one of man's greatest infirmities was the inconsiderate, impersonal way he deals with others. Instead of treating people as "I and thou" where we could be having dialogue, we treat each other as "I and it" and produce monologue. One of my Temple University medical students told me that the average doctor listens to a patient for only about 11 seconds before butting in and judging symptoms or disease. Imagine! One-sixth of a minute.

I was sick of monologue and tired of treating "the mastectomy" or the "gall bladder." I wanted to know the *person* with the illness. My soul longed to bring a semblance of art back into my practice of the science.

Dr. Bernie Siegel entered my life. He was one of *the* prime movers in reintroducing humanism back into medicine. He recoupled the profession back to its noble lineage. Studies show that the goodness and contentment of a physician will be a critical factor in a patient's recovery. Hippocrates espoused this deep truth centuries ago. Bernie lived it.

My ten-year interaction with him started with what I like to call my "Madison experience." My life was changed forever when, upon his invitation, I went to Connecticut and was exposed to more grace and courage than I could ever describe. All types of people from all walks of life faced illness as a challenge, not as a crutch. Their fortitude was encouraging, enlightening and forceful.

I learned how to attempt to make the jump from *curer of diseases* to *healer of illnesses*, from doctor to physician — as distinctly contrasted as black and white.

I learned a great deal from the resentment, fear and anger of those facing their own mortality. They sought traditional treatments of chemotherapy, radiation, and surgery. They also used humor and courage, exercised choice, and took measured risks. All the while they taught each other and anyone else brave enough to truly listen.

What the lessons of illness teach can be beneficial to all. These experiences are the "right stuff" from which can come the achievement of becoming fully human, fully alive.

Exhilarated, I rushed back to Pennsylvania to start a support group with my friend, Rita Miller. S.E.E.K. brought together those with chronic or life-threatening illness who wanted more than traditional therapy. These individuals learned from and taught each other what it took to challenge and defy the odds as they battled their individual maladies. They recognized that life was not always *fair*. There may appear to be no *justice*, but *love* always existed as a resource.

Although Rita and I facilitated this group, we were really the "students." We witnessed genuine miracles as well as physical and spiritual healing. We better understood the difference between wants and needs. Consequently, we changed and grew.

Eight years and many faces have passed, and the group continues to thrive. This book is a testimony to the lessons learned from remarkable people. How to lead a fuller, happier life with some sense of control. How to discover meaning in one's own endeavors. How to recognize that the only purpose in life is to count . . . to have made a positive difference in this world for having lived at all.

It is truly ironic that most of us need to be up against death before we make this connection. Better that we learn later than not at all. I offer you these pages as the distillate of lessons learned from many lives' experiences.

Listen, live, hope, love, cherish!

> Leo G. Frangipane, Jr., M.D.
> November 1995
> Wyomissing, Pennsylvania

Touchstones

Is there a special place in your childhood that gave you great joy and security?

Visit there now in your mind.

Part 1

Centering on Self

Wellsprings

"Sweet mercy is nobility's true badge."

William Shakespeare

Only with the Heart . . .

You have it all wrong. It's backwards.
It should be "You'll see it when you believe it."
Wayne Dyer, author and humanist

Instruction books flood the market. The most popular seem to center on healing. Books by the score are authored by the famous and not-so-famous from Siegel, Cousins, the Simontons and Hay to Dyer, Buscaglia and Dossey. The most worthwhile authors speak of one common element. The initial process of healing, of becoming whole again, starts with peering inward.

Healing is not limited to curing bodily ills. The optimal objective centers upon an attempt to achieve unity and wholeness — physical, mental, emotional, spiritual.

Our feet of clay are rooted in a material world. We are lulled into believing that a high socio-economic standing is our only worthwhile destiny. Hopefully, we eventually come to another realization which grows within us as we change and mature. It speaks to us of a non-material, spiritual realm. This is the world of the mind, the soul, the life-giving spirit.

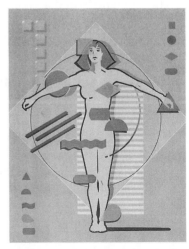

I have operated on thousands of patients and observed every bend and fold of the body. I have yet to find the *soul*. Is it in the heart that beats year after year in unfailing fashion? The legs that carry us from place to place? Is it alive in the wondrous organ we call the brain or the digestive system that processes food we enjoy?

The whole is the sum of the parts, but the organism we call man is much more. The *whole* of the human body can survive very well with far less than the parts inventoried at our birth. Organs can malfunction. Body parts can be removed, yet the organism can remain resilient and vital.

Whatever we name this life force, this "soul," we come to the understanding that it drives and directs the vehicle. "What is essential is invisible to the eye," the Fox says in Saint-Exupéry's *The Little Prince*. "It is only with the heart that one sees rightly."

The mind-body connection is an intricate, intimate, co-dependent relationship. Automobiles can only be directed and useful with a competent driver. In a like manner, the body needs the coupling of a healthy and well-directed spirit.

I do not pretend to understand how this relationship functions, but it does. I have observed courage and fortitude of the mind overcome constraints of the body. I have seen terminally ill people get well. Patients survive circumstances that defy scientific or material explanations. Therefore, I believe that by centering upon the affairs of the unseen, I will discover the clue to becoming truly whole again.

In 1979, a patient I shall call Andrew came to me jaundiced, emaciated and enduring great pain. During surgery I found pancreatic cancer coating bowel, liver and peritoneum. I took several biopsies, confirmed the diagnosis, and closed his abdomen. I could do no more; his disease was so far advanced.

I sat with Andy and his family and said something that I have never said again — to anyone! "Go home, Andy," I haltingly began. "Put your affairs in order. You have six months to live."

How the hell did I know! If I was so smart, why didn't I tell these people tomorrow's lottery number. Well, Andy, went home.

He ate as best he could, prayed a great deal, surrounded himself with his loving family. There were still things he could do. He found the strength to tend to a small garden. He took short walks with friends and waited to see what would happen.

Days became months. Andy's strength and weight began to return. His jaundice slowly disappeared. Thinking this most unusual for a man condemned to die, he nonetheless approached his future cautiously. He expanded his garden, took longer walks, and found himself on the golf course for a few holes.

One day he let me know that unusual things were happening. I received a Hallmark card upon the first anniversary of his diagnosis. "Hi, Dr. Leo. Remember me? Regards, Andrew."

Of course I remembered him! I reached him by phone and asked what was going on. He reminded me that I had sent him home to die, but that it "didn't take." I asked him if he would be so kind as to permit me to do a CAT scan of his abdomen. The x-ray confirmed what my examination led me to suspect. His cancer was gone. The radiologic films were pristine.

I ran up to the pathology lab and loudly complained that the doctors had made a horrible mistake. "It must have been benign pancreatitis or some other problem," I insisted. Otherwise, how could he still be alive from a widely metastatic, highly incurable disease. "This is cancer," they insisted. Everyone agreed, including outside consultants. This was not benign. "Maybe it's a well-behaved malignancy," one of my peers suggested when he heard the story. I asked him what the heck that was, and he had no retort.

I know that was 1979 because this past spring I received the sixteenth anniversary card from Andy. Do I have an explanation for this man's good fortune? No way. But I do know it happened. And I also know that the miracle of this second chance may be related as much to my friend's attitude as to anything that science may attempt to explain.

Andy is deeply religious. He comes from a supportive, loving family. He espouses a philosophy that combines many of the *miracle elements* I will discuss in this book.

First, he understands that when problems come to pass, they rarely come to stay. He recognizes that he is very much in control and a part of the solution to any difficulty he may have to face. He knows that the road to healing starts with looking inward. Likewise, he knows that dying is not a defeat. There are things far worse than dying. Woody Allen adds, "There is something worse than death. If you have ever spent a night with an insurance salesman, you'd know exactly what I mean!"

The following chapters discuss characteristics of survivors, as I see them. People who are unafraid to question. Patients who recognize the necessity for self-examination.

Courage and humility, joy and patience, good humor and love, must begin with self esteem and self love. How can we love anyone else until we love ourselves?

The consequence of these positive qualities is a motivation that directs itself outwardly. The qualities that allow us access to our heart and its life force permit us to see more clearly the heartlights of others. The natural consequence of self-respect and humility, exceptional patients loudly proclaim, is a joyous celebration of life, and it comes to fruition by joining with others. Do something for someone else. Reach out beyond self to others.

The recognition that *I am perfectly capable of becoming whole and I will utilize whatever resources I need to achieve my end* is accomplished quite simply by **faith** in self. The quest for knowledge and understanding starts the cycle.

Faith leads to a kind of desire or **hope**. The materially focused, scientific establishment speaks of this kind of hope as being false, self-defeating, demeaning. There can be no "hope" for those labeled incurable or terminal.

Hope is the fuel of the life force. Without it, meaningful life ceases. What cynics! There is hope, even on the deathbed! Even death can be a great healing. Hope fans the spark of life even at its darkest hour. It allows us to look forward but also reminds us of the joy of the present moment. You are either alive or dead, not living or dying.

The awareness of my being, sprung from the fanned flame of hopeful desire, leads to true understanding of existence. It is through *love* that ultimate knowledge comes. The unconditional love and acceptance that is natural for human beings to desire now becomes easier to give.

And there you have the outline for success. First, recognize the power of what is unseen. Embrace it. Through knowledge gained by faith, hope comes alive and permits self discovery. Finally, ultimate knowledge comes through love. The following chapters discuss methods used by my "incurable" friends to arrive at this point.

Part 2 of this book looks at the natural sequelae of this mechanism: love turned outward. Involvement with others, both adult and child, allows the cycle to become complete. It offers the best opportunity for us to leave our mark.

The formula seems simple. Putting it into action demands great courage and introspection. But to become fully human, to achieve greatness, and to meet challenge with growth are never without difficulty. All of us have the potential to turn these goals into actuality.

I share with you a poem by Leonard Mark Babel that speaks of life and the courage it takes to live under duress. Listen with your heart.

And the Heart of Me Will Flow

I'm willing to accept the facts of whatever this challenge brings.
I plan not to hold myself with bars but only to spread my wings.
It's taken quite a lot of me to get to where I am.
I wish to only be filled with glory and wash away the 'damn'.

I'm willing to take my self-control unchain my aching mind.
To live my life without regret and enjoy this precious time.
I ask that all the anger inside me be released and now set free.
The guilt that's long been making me blind, let my eyes now see.

Feeling sorry for myself will only keep me back.
And continuously crying for hours leaves me only in the black.
I request myself to smile and to look more than just one time.
To unravel any pressing thoughts that could lead me in a bind.

I plan to take each day as one fully lived like there's no tomorrow.
Hold my head with integrity and not drown myself in sorrow.
I forgive myself for whatever I did for what left me sick inside.
To express myself more openly no longer can my truth hide.

Whatever I find that helps me out to feel good about myself.
Will be kept inside my pocket for self-worth can be my wealth.
I shall avoid the negative the people who bring me low.
To strive to be more positive and to let my spirit glow.

Most of all, I'll love myself and be ultimately good to me.
For I am well worth all of this and it's what was meant to be.
Since I can see just how I stand and where I need to go.
I can now let myself go free, the heart of me will flow.

Read,
    listen,
        let your heart flow.

 Wellsprings

"The worst sin towards our fellow creatures is
not to hate them, but to be indifferent to them:
that's the essence of inhumanity."

George Bernard Shaw

Being Responsible

*My breast cancer taught me to care for my son,
because first it taught me to take care of myself.*
Joan, breast cancer survivor, mother of a
profoundly disabled teenage son

 I have a substitute for morphine. Sit for awhile in a hospital lounge, doctor's reception room, auto repair shop or airport terminal. Pick up one of their *current* (translated: 1987) *Reader's Digests* on the table next to you. Instant narcolepsy! Once restlessness and frustration pass, I am lulled into boredom and numb all over. There is something about waiting for the "experts" to take care of our problems that strips our minds of control.

We need to be more aware of the ways we are ignored, manipulated and dehumanized by people and institutions. Their behavior gives them dominance and control over us if we slip into passive, submissive roles.

Manipulation is effective, too. We are told, "Here. Take off your clothes and put this on." The nurse hands you an illusion in minimalism — an awful, flapping-in-the-wind, hospital gown. Like robots, we readily obey. Not one in ten thousand will balk.

I recently "walked a mile in my patients' slippers" when I found myself at the other end of the scalpel for hip surgery. The hospital gown defines territory. I felt bare, open, vulnerable. What was privately mine, now belonged to anyone whose wondering eyes were unfortunate enough to catch sight of my bony knees and dimpled . . ., you get the picture! It was humbling and made me feel very inferior. Hospital gowns do an excellent job of putting you in your place and preparing you to placidly follow the rules and listen to the "experts."

No one complains. Everyone behaves and does as told. We settle into the compliant, unquestioning patient mode. Hospital gowns have become the patient's white — or pink or blue — flag of surrender. Cripes! You are stark naked below the thigh and a breeze is fanning your fanny — hardly a dress-for-success model.

My Gram' Mary was the master of directive counseling — the Queen and ruler. Four foot ten of pure Sicilian power, she raised a large extended family. When she shouted, "Jump!" we all cried, "How high?" Gram' thought little of doctors and hospitals. They were there for *other people*. Wear your garlic, put red sauce on just about everything, and you won't have much need of the medical profession. Actually, I have always suspected there was something very therapeutic about tomato sauce with fresh basil. As for the garlic, we never caught anything communicable since nobody dared come too close!

In her mid sixties, Mary showed signs of having an enlarged thyroid. Reluctantly, she went to a surgeon after homemade remedies and prayers to St. Anthony did not work. Her surgeon matter-of-factly told her how he intended to operate on her neck and remove the diseased gland. Mary's eyes widened. She informed the startled doctor that he was not going to "slit my neck and remove something God put there for a purpose." Her Sicilian blood slowly started to boil. The word *intimidation* was not part of her vocabulary.

A bit surprised by the spunk of this little lady (half naked thanks to the lovely exam gown), the doctor verbally traipsed through landmines. "But you're too old to fool around with this," he implored.

"Too old! 'Too old' did you say?!" He had managed to become entangled in one of Grams' most revered topics. "Remember, the best music is played on old instruments," she proclaimed and exited leaving an astonished surgeon to ponder her words.

She lived three decades longer, thyroid intact and unchanged. Her treatment? Daily virgin olive oil, Italian bread, hot red pepper and generous portions of sauteed garlic. This may very well be the perfect cure for goiter (not bad for bowels either).

Mary never gave a second thought to believing she was a participant in her own health care. Her longevity was proof. "If the doctor and I don't see eye to eye," she would remark, "I'll get a stool to stand on." She felt the medical profession was wonderful and devoted but human like her. She felt that some doctors needed to become more human and exposed themselves.

Now wait a minute! If every patient demanded special consideration and did as they darn well pleased, the whole system might break down. Would that be good for business? Well, is good business always good medicine?

An anecdotal study was done years ago on cancer patients by one of our most prestigious teaching hospitals. What effect did patient attitude and behavior have on the immune system? Could certain feelings and emotions alter one's ability to fend off illness? There was a hint in those days that chronic illness and malignancy might somehow be linked and affected by attitude. The supposition was, quite rightly, that the link occurred in the body's own watchdog, the immune system.

There was a serious flaw in the study, however. The patient subjects were never interviewed directly even though their thoughts and actions were crucial to the study! Researchers relied entirely on the objective assessments of the doctors and nurses who were treating these people.

Based on staff assessments, researchers split the patients into two groups. One group included the long-suffering, never-complaining who accepted treatment without question and regardless of side effects. These were the "good" patients, the saints who would never think of pressing the call button for a bedpan even when their teeth were floating. They went along with the system, and "Don't Rock the Boat" was their motto.

The second group's theme song seemed to be "I Did It My Way." They complained all the time about everything. Interestingly, this behavior group was only one-tenth the number of the first group. These folks did not like the food and grumped every time they were awakened to take a sleeping pill. They would not go to x-ray for a test or take a pill unless someone explained (horrors!) what it was for or what it was supposed to do.

They demanded to see their doctors now, if not sooner. Most caregivers avoided them and the thousand questions that had to be answered before extrication from their rooms was possible. They invariably got labeled "difficult" or "noncompliant" right on their charts. (Imagine my Gram's office records!) Too often they were labeled as being in denial or accused of being irrational even unbalanced. How contrary and pesky could they be?!

At the conclusion of the study, what the researchers found surprised even them. Patients with the highest levels of immunity were the ones who *misbehaved* the most, as judged by the staff. Those with the lowest level of immune activity were the compliant and well behaved ones. In addition to living longer, the cranks also enjoyed a better quality of life than did the saints.

The study was an eye opener. In the years since, this area of study has generated an enormous flurry of research. Science has come to accept the fact that the mind, the brain, the soul, the seat of intelligence, the living spirit, the life-giving force — no matter what it is called — has a real role in the physical realm of disease. The mind-body connection is no longer a theory. It is fact. Attitude makes an enormous difference in outcome for the terminally ill or people with heart disease, AIDS, other modern life afflictions, and even the common cold. Our ability to defeat and stave off illness starts with our attitude toward that disease.

———————•———————

We are not our illness. The microbe that causes disease flourishes in the fertile petri dish of self-doubt, depression, anger, resentment and fear. The entire field of psycho-neuro-immunology explores these connections. It is through "neurotransmitters" that we physically become what we think. Researchers at UCLA have proven this theory and they and Norman Cousins have written about it.

I tell you, we are what we eat. We become what we ingest. In my practice, I know where those *Nutty Buddies* and *Twinkies* find their way. Why can't we believe what the Roman historian and philosopher, Aurelius, stated centuries ago: "We are what we think. We become what we perceive."

When I make comments like these, which I do with growing frequency, I find myself labeled *new age, holistic, born again* or *homeopathic*. I'm not sure what all these tags mean. Frankly, I do not care what people call my practice. I like to think of it as the art of loving the patient, bringing the craft of medicine back into the twentieth century.

I grew up with labels. "Dago" or "Wop" hurt at first. It took a unique set of loving parents and grandparents, and lots of others in my personal support system, to set me straight. Labels hurt if we allow them to inhibit, restrict or wound. They are used to categorize what others cannot understand. Did those who called me "Wop" know me? Did they know what special times I had with my family such as the beautiful Sunday dinners? Did they begin to understand how loved the "Dago" kid felt when times of joy or sorrow came to our home? I doubt it.

I am where I am and who I am as the result of a personal transformation spanning more than 20 years of being a doctor. The greater part of this time has been spent trying to integrate Life with what I have absorbed in my professional training, years of medical school, internship, residency and private practice.

I have learned there is a quantum leap between being a doctor and becoming a physician. It is as different as biologically starting a child and to being a loving, nurturing, involved father. Anyone with proper training can doctor a disease. Getting the letters, M.D. at the end of one's name does not magically impart the deeper substance of the profession. Doctors are great healers, but so too was my grandmother.

The essence of physicianship lies in understanding the *feelings* of patients and how these translate into *needs*. Feelings are important because they tell of *wants*. To discover base line emotions, one must spend time, listen, and get involved. Qualification cannot be done through numbers. "Congratulations! You are now a legitimate Doctor because you've seen 162.7 patients. You qualify!" No, because each individual, each patient is different, unique, one of a kind.

Most parents do not have trouble grasping this concept. Each of their children is different. Doctors are another story. For one thing, individualization of patients has not been taught — or at least not taught well — in medical schools. There is so much to learn, and most schools concentrate on details and processes, the *science* of medicine.

Additionally, the high degree of specialization in modern medicine puts patients in neat little boxes labeled with various body parts. We lose sight of the *whole* person. Go to the ENT doctor for ears, nose and throat problems. Don't ask about gall bladder or spleen. They are not in his box.

As a surgical specialist, I have often heard patients referred to as "the gall bladder" or "the mastectomy" reflecting back to what Buber said about *I, Thou* and *It*. How can we hope to have any credible, loving relationship with patients if we continually treat them as "Its"? Treating people as "What" instead of "Who" may be the most efficient way of dealing with busy medical schedules. It also is a most effective and mind-numbing method of putting distance between us and the life and death matters we deal with daily. Perhaps the next step is bar coding patients so they can be scanned before being slid onto the production line.

I hear some of my colleagues say they do not care to "love" the patient. They are simply doing a job, performing a service. So does the local dry cleaner! Personally, I need a physician who wants to treat my body, soul, mind and spirit! Let him or her understand that part of my problem may have as much to do with my attitude as with my microbes.

After a thousand gall bladder and a thousand more mastectomy operations, how can a physician avoid looking at the face in the mirror and asking, "Why do I really do what I do? Is it the money, prestige, influence? Was there once another higher, more noble reason? Where along the way did I push it into the background?"

For me, it all became apparent one day when a gentle, elderly lady entered my office. I had removed her diseased gall bladder two weeks earlier. She had done well and was soon discharged. As often happened, I was not the doctor doing rounds during her two-day stay. So, except for the operation during which she was out cold, I had had no contact with her. Later, when she came for her office visit, I welcomed her and asked how she felt. She politely answered that she was fine, but "Who are you?"

Who was I! Incredulous, my mind flashed with answers. I was the one who deftly incised her body. I was the one who had painstakingly removed diseased tissue! I had saved her life! Who, by golly, was I! Then it all hit me. Had my patients become faceless objects!?

I looked into her kindly, trusting eyes. I did not see the body, I did not see the cancer, I did not see the charts and flapping hospital gown. I saw her soul, her person, her self. I saw what I should have been seeing all along. I saw what I had been losing as a physician.

"Who are you?" she had asked. Indeed, I could not answer.

This experience changed my life. At the end of much soul-searching, I decided to move on. My high-pressure but nonetheless regimented and impersonal work situation needed overhauling. I found a personally satisfying, small solo practice to be the answer. The tricky part was trying to integrate what I knew about medicine with everything else I knew about life, which then seemed like damned little.

———◆———

Everyone has an Uncle Henry, a cantankerous, combative, demanding old coot who has had one foot in the grave and the other on a banana peel for so long we are convinced he will bury us all.

My training as a doctor did not explore the Uncle Henrys of the world. What if he was on to something? Was there something in his contrary nature that kept him alive and kicking? If you could distill and bottle it, wouldn't you? You'd have the hottest prescription drug on the market.

Conversely, what about the people who seem to lack any fight at all and slip off so suddenly and seemingly too easily?

Two men worked in the same office. Both had bad tickers and both had pressure cooker jobs. Their outlook on life, however, was a contrast in opposites. Brad's job meant everything to him. He prided himself on his work ethic — 14-hour days, lunch at his desk, Saturdays at the office. It is understandable that his first massive heart attack put him in a real bind. When he returned to work, he continued in his old job though he was no longer able to meet its demands. As you can well imagine, he was under enormous stress. He did not go to his boss about reducing his workload. No sir! He absolutely refused to consider reassignment to a less intense position, and he positively refused to consider early disability retirement. "I'm not a quitter. I'm not a complainer!"

Bart was equally a type A. But when The-Almost-Big-One took him out of commission for awhile, he made darn sure everyone in the office knew his plight. As he put it, "Yes, sir, it's like a walking time bomb in my chest. Could go off at any minute!" He brought his own doctor's bag to work each day. It looked just like the real thing with an amazing array of pill bottles, a blood pressure cuff and stethoscope. Various medications would be taken with theatrical flourish at regular intervals throughout his workshift. He did not come in when the weather was especially rotten. If he felt sick, he called off work in a heartbeat. After establishing his case beyond a doubt, he demanded and obtained early disability retirement.

It is now twenty years later. Bart is approaching 80 and still telling everyone about the bomb in his chest. Only now he does it coast to coast and on two continents. He enjoys a very active retired life. Oh, he still breaks appointments depending on how he feels, but he does so without guilt or shame. "I will not kill myself for anyone, or any reason. If you don't look out for yourself, nobody will do it for you."

Brad? He didn't live to collect a dime of Social Security. He died eight months shy of 61.

Monday, 9:00 a.m. is no joke. That's when most on-the-job heart attacks occur. Interesting.

Do we hate our jobs that much? Are we driven by guilt or obligation instead of any sense of self love, accomplishment and meaning?

One benefit of the so called "new age" movement may be to bring this introspection to the forefront of our consciousness. Look after yourself, love yourself, and center upon who you are and what you want to become.

Gram' Mary had her priorities straight. I learned from her to do what I want but not in a selfish, self-serving way. She exercised choice. Given the choice between going shopping with me and Mom or helping a friend with an errand, there was no decision. Her family, her personal enjoyment would come first if she chose. Don't get me wrong. She was a kind and generous person, but she realized that her "yes" had no value if she didn't exercise her right to say "no."

I am in awe of the power of attitude.

Those of you who experienced the winter of 1993-94 in the Northeast know it was not an easy time. It snowed almost daily and was well below freezing days on end. Pipes froze. Roofs collapsed. Cars, if they could be dug out of snow banks, wouldn't start. And then, God threw in an earthquake, a rarity where I live!

My wife, Joyce, and I decided, "Enough!" and headed south to enjoy some sun. I was buying a hat for our intended trip, when I spied a baseball cap whose legend on the front proclaimed, "Having a bad hair day." From the back of the hat hung a long ponytail available in a variety of colors. Before I tell you that I sprung for the $1.29 and bought one, I must 'fess up. I have a forehead that extends all the way to the back of my head. Well, when I found a cap with a ponytail that matched what is left of the fringe above my ears, you will see why I could not resist.

Joyce and I had great fun with my new hat. I looked like a Woodstock groupie. All I needed to complete the getup were love beads, a lava lamp, and an incense pot. Hat on head and pony tail flapping, I arrived at the airport. Joyce left for the ladies' room. Content and casual, I sat reading a magazine and oblivious to the rest of the world until I felt the stare of a well-dressed couple across from me. Only then did it dawn on me that they must have noticed my chapeau. I knew what they were thinking. Here is an aging, pot-smoking, 60's flower child lost forever in a personal hallucinogenic time warp — just the kind of guy they would love to see board anybody's flight but theirs.

Still, I kept the cap on, returning their looks with smiles. At just the right moment, I slipped it off with junior-high cool. Boy, did their attitudes change! When I wore the hairy cap, they were ready to write me off at a glance. Without it, I looked like any normal, average, middle-aged, guy heading off for a vacation. A lawyer, maybe, or even a doctor! Who could tell? Once they realized the joke was on them, they gave me shy, embarrassed smiles.

That hat is now a featured part of the talks I give about the power of attitude. Nothing I can think of illustrates better how easy it is to misjudge people.

No audience I have addressed understands "perception" better than the guests and staff at Rainbow Home, a local AIDS hospice. It is difficult for most of us to think of anything worse than the disease AIDS. To those who suffer and to those who have the compassion and courage to treat them, the social stigma is far worse. It is a modern day leprosy.

The reception I received when I walked into Rainbow Home wearing my cap with the ponytail is very different from elsewhere. These folks did not bat an eye. They tolerated me as I appeared. They listened to what I had to say without prejudgment. When I eventually got around to removing it, the joint broke up. Their laughter underscored the point: "Why worry about what people think?"

Our upbringing and genes lead us to please and to seek favor and approval from others. Whether in family, community or workplace, it is important and essential to get along. If everyone went his or her own way without care or concern for anyone else, we would all be walking around with boom boxes blasting instead of just the few louts who do.

It is true that worrying about what other people think is a great moral force — good old peer and societal pressure. But, when guilt and shame kill AIDS patients more quickly than the disease itself, the consequence is too much! There comes a time when our well being, maybe even our survival, is at stake. If we cannot take a stand for our basic rights and the values we hold dear, then we do not stand a chance. The truth is that simple, that profound.

———————

I am annoyed by patients who passively slump in my office chair as I explain their diagnosis and treatment options. When they answer, "Fix me." or "Do whatever you think best," I want to shout, "Don't do this to yourself! Take charge of your life! It's the only way. Be part of the solution, not part of the problem!"

If they really want to be "fixed," I am tempted to recommend they see the local veterinarian, the neutering clinic, or the auto body shop. I don't, of course. I wish I could enable each passive, hopeless person to see how important an attitude adjustment is to their vitality and healing. It has been my experience that only one in ten patients actively accepts the challenge by being a responsible participant in their disease or illness. Sad. I crusade and rally to counteract the negative. I try to change attitudes wherever I can, in auditoriums full of people or just one lost soul at a time.

I wish everyone would think like my friend, Harriet who is up in years, but unstoppably forward and direct. She told me once that she had to "break in a new doctor." He listened to her complaints, the usual infirmities of age. Then she told this new chap what she expected of him in trying to help her overcome some of her difficulties.

"Madam," he responded with a smirk, "I am a doctor, not a magician." To her eternal credit, Harriet immediately put him in his place. "You just dispense the medicine," she snapped, "and I'll supply the magic!"

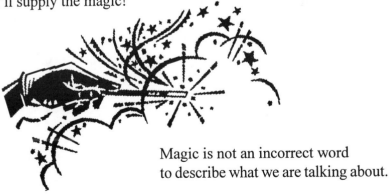

Magic is not an incorrect word
to describe what we are talking about.

Rita Miller, one of the first facilitators of our cancer support group, has a bon mots which she borrowed from Bernie Siegel.

She told clients that she wanted them to become resp-pants a combination of "responsible" and "participant." Rita lent the word to me and I have been using it ever since.

To me the word resp-pant says it all. Find out what is happening. Do not blindly accept dictates. Decide for yourself. Above all, fight for your life! Forget that the word "patient" comes from the Latin root meaning "to submit." Do not be submissive! Be a responsible participant instead.

Demand little things. Ask to be treated with kindness. Use phrases such as: Explain things to me. ... What do you mean by that? ... Are there any other options? ... I'd like the bed by the window with the beautiful view. ... I want to go around the ward in my jogging suit. It's more comfortable, okay?

While you are thinking of other simple statements you can make to take back some control in your life, I will tell you another story.

Joan was in her early 20's when she came to my office with a lump in her breast. She was terrified. My first guess was that it was benign. I told her a biopsy would be the only way to know for sure. Anxiously, she agreed. I was wrong. The diagnosis was cancer. Joan proved to be an exceedingly emotional and difficult patient. But remember, this behavior is good. We spent hours discussing options. She made her choices and did not look back.

In cases like Joan, it is not wise to become pregnant afterwards. Hormonal changes that accompany pregnancy could hasten recurrence, like throwing fertilizer on malignant cells, some researchers believe. Don't do it, we advised. Yet Joan and her husband wanted badly to have a child. It was her choice.

She gave birth to a healthy son, her "miracle baby." Sadly, while still a baby, Andrew suffered a high fever that caused profound, brain damage. Today he is a teenager who

recognizes no one. He has dozens of seizures daily. Even though her son demands full-time attention, Joan still lovingly regards him as her miracle baby. She says her cancer was a gift in disguise. It allowed her to appreciate her wonderful son. "My breast cancer taught me to care for my son, because first it taught me to take care of myself," she says.

It is my patients who have taught me. Minor operations no longer require a hospital gown. A comfortable sweatsuit does just fine. There is no increased risk of infection or anything else except maybe the increased risk of patient ease and comfort.

If you cannot stand that elevator music they sometimes play in the operating room, I usually come armed with tapes and CDs for your listening pleasure. The *DJ Doc* one patient called me. I'll even sing to you, much to the chagrin of the nurses. I do a great Mario Lanza or equally good Neil Diamond. Everyone agrees I should still keep my day job though.

There were never increased risks of horrible, unsanitary, do-not-draw-outside-the-lines repercussions as a result of my being patient-centered. If I break a rule, I see the looks and hear the whispers, just like the times I wear the cap with the ponytail. Who cares? If wearing their own clothes makes patients feel more comfortable, more relaxed and in control, then for me, it is good medicine. And that is all that matters in the end. Isn't it?

Touchstones

If your house caught fire and you could only rescue three things, what would they be?

It's the Trip

My daddy told me that there is no more yesterday.
And tomorrow isn't here yet.
But that I should live my life to-now.

Jason, my 8 year old friend with leukemia

South Philadelphia was a slice of the United Nations. Our brownstone, three-story walk-up stood sentry like *The Winged Victory of Samothrace.* For me, grey sidewalks ended and life began at this three-generation home shared by Mom, Dad and my maternal grandparents. Cousins and assorted relatives lived within walking distance. Since coming from Italy, 13th Street was home to my grandparents.

Talk about convenient! It was great being related to so many instant playmates! Adventure was the operative word in this dynamic, bustling neighborhood containing our big, old house which held my extended family. Add aunts, uncles, cousins and numerous pets — instant support system!

Aromas wafted from our house and made people drool from blocks away. Autumn brought simmering red sauce, robust with garlic and basil. Zinfandel wine being pressed in the basement intoxicated the air of a summer's day. Tomato plants, peppers and squash tendrilled and burst to abundance, trailing halfway to Broad Street from Grandfather's garden tucked in the back yard. A fig tree, pruned and protected, grew in a corner. Rows of brownstones, loving relatives, wonderful smells, Phillies baseball, the music of Bandstand . . .

When I was about Jason's age, I couldn't wait for the first week in August for Dad's vacation. We would head to the shore, a magical place where we escaped from school, chores and routine life. From mid June I'd pester my parents, "When are we going? When are we leaving? Is it August yet?"

Then *the* Saturday finally rolled around. We loaded the 1955 Chevy station wagon chock full of life's belongings. The "Woody," with real wood panelling, was packed to the hilt and groaned as Dad managed to close the back hatch. We headed east leaving behind ten thousand friends and relatives who lived on our block. To the beach!

All the way it was, "Are we there yet? Are we there yet?" And then that glorious block where roads ended and endless hot sand rippled down to crashing waves. We arrived and unpacked — an escape from urban life for one solid week's adventure in the sun. And whom should we meet on the boardwalk and beach? At least half of the ten thousand people we tried to leave behind in South Philly!!

As I "grew up," anticipation never measured up to reality. There were always too many mosquitoes or biting flies. Afternoon rains spoiled beach plans. The week never quite lived up to the anticipation of getting there. What a disappointment!

Remember the Peggy Lee song, "Is That All There Is?"? Now I understand her message. The most exciting part of an event is often the anticipation, not the event itself. I remember being melancholy on Christmas, perhaps I realized it was here and soon would be gone. Celebrating birthdays, anniversaries and holidays brought a tinge of unhappiness upon their arrival. Weeks of preparation and tingling excitement appeared to be the best part of any event. Listen to the words of Robert Hastings:

The Station

*Tucked away in our subconscious is an idyllic vision.
We see ourselves on a long trip that spans the continent.
We are traveling by train. Out the windows we drink in the
passing scene of cars on nearby highways, of children waving
at a crossing, of cattle grazing on a distant hillside, of smoke
pouring from a power plant, of row upon row of corn and
wheat, of flatlands and valleys, of mountains and rolling
hillsides, of city skylines and village halls. But uppermost in
our minds is the final destination. On a certain day at a
certain hour we will pull into the station. Bands will be
playing and flags waving. Once we get there so many
wonderful dreams will come true and the pieces of our
lives will fit together like a completed jigsaw puzzle.*

*How restlessly we pace the aisles, cursing the minutes for
loitering — waiting, waiting, waiting for the station.*

*"When we reach the station that will be it!" we cry.
"When I'm 18!"
"When I buy a new 450SL Mercedes."
"When I put the last kid through college."
"When I pay off the mortgage."
"When I get a promotion."
"When I reach retirement age, I shall live happily ever after."*

*We need to realize there is no station, no one place to arrive at
once and for all. The true joy of life is the trip. The station is
only a dream. It constantly outdistances us.*

*"Relish the moment" is a good motto, especially when coupled
with Psalm 118:24. — "This is the day the Lord has made; we
will rejoice and be glad in it." It isn't the burdens of today
that drive men mad. It is the regrets over yesterday and the
fear of tomorrow. Regret and fear are twin thieves who rob
us of today.*

*So stop pacing the aisles and counting the miles. Instead,
climb more mountains. Eat more ice cream. Go barefoot more
often. Swim more rivers. Watch more sunsets. Laugh more.
Cry less. Life must be lived as we go along.*

The station will come soon enough.

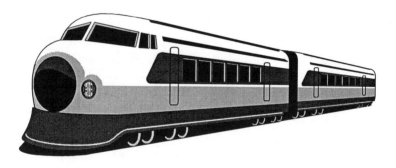

Children are eternally waiting for something. As kids we are
told we are not quite *old enough* for many things we desired.
Sometimes we were even denied answers to questions until we
grew up. Our upbringing led us to believe that life was going to
be much better some day, just as soon as we reach that elusive,
shifting "old enough." Old enough to do what? Drive? Date?
Go to rock concerts? Get out of high school? Smoke? Drink?
Vote? Make big money? Get a fast car? Move out on our own?
Not have to answer to Mom anymore? Be an adult?

With everything always to be looked forward to in anticipation, it is no wonder kids are bored with the here and now and why they can sit in a houseful of toys and games and say, "I have nothing to do."

We still cling to the same patterns. Long after we leave our childhood, we continue to always look forward and to forget about the *now*. But, as adults, childhood expectations are replaced by worry.

I am not sure I know what makes an *adult* . . . well, an *adult*. I know it is not just being old enough to vote. And I am certain it is not when you get a job. For sure it is not marriage or the responsibilities of parenthood. Is it when we start looking back on childhood as the best time of our life?

When do we become an *adult*? To me, maturity occurs when we start living in the *now* and are not distracted by what the future will bring. This insight is not something I learned on my own. Just hang around a group of terminally ill people, and you will quickly realize your shrinking priorities are precious few. One of these is living in the moment. Now.

Take my eight-year old friend, Jason, who had leukemia. His only hope was a dangerous and difficult procedure involving high dose chemotherapy and bone marrow transplants. If all went well, Jason would be home in 40 to 45 days from his isolation unit at Children's Hospital in Philadelphia.

Jason's daddy had just heard Bernie Siegel speak at a workshop where Siegel told the story of a similar child with leukemia. So he encouraged Jason to fill that long and often lonely time writing to friends, drawing pictures, and making little gifts. I am fortunate to be counted as one of Jason's buddies. He sent me a large picture he had drawn of me in my office. He saw me not quite as I am. He envisioned a tall, svelte man with a crop of curly brown hair completely covering his head! Oh, to see through the eyes of children.

Needless to say, I was deeply touched. This loving portrait graced my refrigerator door for months for all to see and admire. There was a note on the picture in blue crayon and childish scrawl.

> Dr. Leo,
> My daddy told me there is no more yesterday.
> And that tomorrow isn't here yet.
> But that I should live my life to-now.

To-now, not today. That certainly pins it down to the moment, doesn't it? What a tough concept to grasp! Our memories keep yesterdays as fresh as todays. Our imaginations create futures just as vivid as the present. They all flow in our mind in a swirling, continuous stream. We are equipped to easily paddle upstream or down or drift in the eddies at will. This behavior is precisely what we do when we are overcome with nostalgia or get lost in daydreams. Our thoughts envision romance, adventure and riches when we cash in that big lottery ticket.

As hard as we try to compartmentalize our world, we cannot. "Tomorrow," Annie sings, "is always a day away." This might have been a sad, wistful lament, but not the way it was written. It is actually an upbeat show stopper that defines Annie as the eternal optimist. She keeps her hopes alive. She is able to go out of her way to raise the spirits of unfortunate wretches who cross her path. Is Annie pure fantasy, totally unrealistic? It would take Mother Theresa to stand up to all the perils Annie's plot lines place her in. Any kid and most adults would be crushed by them.

So it's been said, but it's just not so.

Not much can happen to a kid that is worse than leukemia. Yet

Jason persevered, sick to death from the devastating chemo-therapy, kept in isolation, and wondering if he would ever leave the hospital alive. Yet he was still capable of raising the spirits and touching the heart of a bald, bigger than svelte friend. How? By living his life to-now.

Cancer devastates. Yet, in the cancer support groups that are a vital part of my medical practice, there is very little sadness. Even though everyone is facing his or her own imminent mortality, these brave people learn to deal with it. Even though death continually culls through the membership rolls, these individuals survive. How? They do it like Jason, by focusing on to-now without regretting yesterdays or worrying about tomorrows.

I encourage group clients to do four things:
- **Keep a journal and write down your feelings.**
  Feelings speak of needs and tell us how to
  best solve current problems.
- **Be active in your support group.**
  Participate in whatever group it takes to give you
  affirmation and constructive criticism or challenge.
  That might be a church group, an organization like
  S.E.E.K. or your family.
- **Get in touch with yourself through imaging,**
  prayer or meditation.
- **Live to-now.**
  This requirement is the toughest of all.

These are exercises that can be done, but mostly this is a "you're on your own" syllabus.

To someone who has not been through such an experience, these exercises may sound like an impossible task. It may appear un-realistic, a head-in-the-sand approach to a dire, life-threatening situation. It is not. In fact, it is exactly the opposite. Treatment alternatives and prognosis probabilities are openly discussed. Ideas for taking care of practical matters after death are brought up. Some write memory books, poems or epitaphs, others shoot videotapes to leave for younger generations. Each death is mourned. But, life goes on one day at a time.

What still amazes me is the enthusiasm my patient-friends manage to put into each day. They look at me so hard! One of the greatest compliments any of us can receive is the favor of really being listened to. My friends listen so intensely that they sometimes intimidate me! We are all told to live each day as if it might be our last, but I've never met anyone who appreciates those words more than the terminally ill. They somehow remain full of hope and appreciative beyond words, recognizing that while life is difficult, "fairness" is a relative term. In spite of there being no perceived justice, there is love and hope.

One young mother who had undergone a mastectomy, chemotherapy and radiation found herself gazing out her kitchen window. She sobbed as she observed the snow-covered fields. "I saw beauty," she explained. It was not regrets. She was not sad at the thought she might never see snow again. Nor was it anger or resentment that her life might be cut short. It was pure joy. "I had never taken the time to notice how beautiful a snowy night could be."

You dip into the cool, running water of the stream and enjoy its freshness. You remove your hand and moments later plunge it in again. Your hand is in a different place. The water that touched you is far downstream. The pleasure of the second experience is new and now.

My friends will tell you, whether asked or not, that they are better persons for their illness and that their disease has made life better by instructing them to live each day to the fullest. "I live my life urgently, not wasting any time," stated one such individual. These exceptional people view their problems not as something separate from their lives, not as their murderer but as another life event to be experienced and even appreciated. "What can this evil thing possibly teach me" is often their attitude.

I learned this lesson from my own private tutor one night. It was very late, and I hurried through hospital halls frantically trying to get caught up on my rounds. I was tired, frustrated and angry. Nothing was going the way I had hoped. In the midst of my mania, an older colleague came up to me. This compassionate physician took a few minutes to pass on some good and free advice. "Leo," he said. "You can only do one thing well at a time."

That is all he said, but it was just at the right moment. Medicine is about people, not about keeping pretty charts. It is about holding hands and smiling, not just treating illnesses or prescribing drugs. It's about listening and compassion, not just trips to the operating room and discussions of interesting cases.

One of my heroic friends with non-treatable ovarian cancer spoke up at a group meeting. "You know," she said, "I used to start preparing the family's Fourth of July picnic weeks ahead of time. I'd work up elaborate menus and worry what we would do if the weather was bad. Now that I have cancer, I do not have the time to waste planning. There are so many other things I would rather do with my days. So this year I think I will put off planning for this year's picnic till the third of July."

So, I think, will I.

**The supreme happiness in life is
the conviction that we are loved.**
Victor Hugo, *Les Miserables*

Aging with Grace

*Surround yourself with people who keep
their minds full but their bowels empty.*
Billy Reifsnyder, then 99, on the secrets of life.

Georgetown Medical School, Washington, D.C.

My niece, fulfilling her life's dream, was graduating. She and
200 other new doctors spoke the Hippocratic Oath. In my mind,
I sentimentally revisited Temple University where the words had
come from my heart through my lips 23 years ago. This little girl
who could barely walk when I first met her aunt, my wife, was
now a beautiful young lady. I recalled how I had held her, watched
her grow, struggle and succeed. Where had the years gone? Had
I walked the graduation stage just yesterday?

Nobody wants to be old. Teeth fall out. Your body falls apart.
Your kids get wrapped up in their own lives. Your
spouse dies and your friends move away or die,
too. Your old neighborhood has changed
so much there is nobody left who remembers you. You even have trouble remem-
bering things yourself. We avoid getting
older by all machinations. The only alternative is to die young, and who wants that?

Today, people live decades past retirement and

watch youth disappear under wrinkles, aches and pains. We can exercise — a good thing if you are going to live a long life. We can color our hair, get face lifts, and use wrinkle creams and makeup to hide the ravages of aging. We can stay younger looking and remain active through our 70s, 80s and even 90s. But we still get older.

A man well into his ninth decade told me that it takes a great deal of bravery to grow old, to get up each morning with purpose, goal and direction, knowing that many friends and even our children have left through death. Most of us are not prepared for the concept of getting older, he states, because we thought it would somehow happen to the other person, not us. Physicians, especially surgeons, do not have that luxury. We see a lot of older people because they are the ones who most often get sick.

In my boyhood home, death was discussed openly, not whispered. Death was a part of life. Getting older meant you might die sooner. So living was all the more important! People were born in our house and died in our house. The parlor was the place adults and children came to pay last respects to the deceased.

Today we shelter young people from "natural" death to the point where youngsters avoid the elderly, yet our society condones violent death in its mass media. We see people die in horrific ways each day on the news and "entertainment" communications. We sit and stare. In real life, *Throw Away* is the name of the game. Put Grandma or Grandpa in a nursing home. Many can not be bothered accepting the responsibility of eldercare.

People die in nursing homes, I am certain, because they do not get enough love and interaction. Excellent medical care is not enough. Do not water a plant or a flower for a few weeks and watch what happens. Well, the same goes for people.

All of us are guilty of avoiding the elderly. Maybe we don't want to listen to a litany of gripes and pains or "the way things were." A good physician will turn a keen ear toward the older population to find out what is really wrong and what is needed to help them survive and thrive. When we take the time to listen, the rewards are immense. Yes, we can determine a diagnosis but we can also glean insight and wisdom about life. Who better to tell us than those who have experienced the most of it. If we listen with our hearts, we can hear the lessons of age.

———— ● ————

Despite its aggravations, getting older allows multiple opportunities for challenge, growth and change. I recently read in the newspaper with great interest of a gentleman who wanted to celebrate his ninetieth birthday by bungee jumping from a tower. This would not exactly be my first desire, but hey, if that is his wish, why not! He needed a doctor's signature before the bungee jumping people would grant permission.

Doctor after doctor told him, "You're too old! You'll hurt yourself!" One even said that there were "surer, faster and less painful ways to commit suicide." Undaunted, our advanced Evil Knevil found a physician who could find no reason not to permit him this thrill. He was in great shape physically, was prepared by various exercises to attempt the jump, and was aware of the possible danger. "Go for it," he said.

With that, the man jumped, had a wonderful time, and walked away unharmed. He did say it was his first and last time, however.

———•———

An 80-year old lady came to me several years ago with a suspicious breast lump. She was realistic about her future should this be bad news. However, she insisted no one would stop her from the gift her grandchildren had given her for her birthday. Her biopsy surgery must be delayed for a week until she took her hot air balloon ride on her birthday. I said, "Of course!" She took her ride and all during her biopsy, done under local anesthesia, she regaled me with the thrills of her glorious adventure.

I was reminded by an elderly woman that Michelangelo was well over seventy when he painted the Sistine Chapel ceiling. Amazing! I don't even like to climb a ladder to clean rain gutters, and I am a lot younger than the great artist was when he climbed that scaffolding. Imagine lying under that ceiling with brushes and paints for endless hours to produce one of the world's most glorious masterpieces. Michelangelo may have been old, but he refused to be trapped into acting or thinking old.

Grandma Moses did not even take up art until her 70s. Of 1,500 pictures she completed, five hundred were done after her 100th year. Goethe wrote *Faustus* at the age of 80. George Bernard Shaw, at the age of 96, broke his hip when he fell out of an apple tree he had been pruning! Duke Ellington, when passed over for a prestigious music award in his late 60s responded, "God didn't want me to be too famous too soon in my life."

Those were well-known, historical characters, but we can find plenty of everyday older folks with similar vitality and closer to home. One of the most revered persons in my neck of the woods was Gene Shirk, two-time mayor of Reading, Pennsylvania. His long, illustrious, nonstop career included teaching, coaching, being a college athletic director, and being involved in numerous civic, cultural and religious affairs. In his 90s, Gene still served as chairperson for the local community television and hosted several programs including a weekly "Generation Gap" featuring discussions with high school students.

He still coached cross country at Albright College and was the oldest active collegiate coach in the nation. At the age of 92, on the weekend before he died, he made his theatrical debut with his wife in a two-character play. Never sick a day in his life, his death was a shock to the entire community. Gene died in an auto accident on his way to meet friends for lunch and bowling. While tragic, it was somehow fitting to think that he died busy.

Then there's Billy.

Billy Reifsnyder sauntered into my office slightly bent, using a cane, but nonetheless spry and alert. His red plaid hunting shirt framed his lined, wise face. A narrow, 14-karat smile, displayed often, showed numerous gaps where teeth left no forwarding address. Blue striped suspenders stretched under the pull of yesteryear's full-cut trousers.

He was accompanied by his son, Norman, a man in his seventies. If Norm was that old, how old was the father?! "99 years young!" I was told. Hard of hearing, Billy still understood as I explained his medical predicament. He had a colon tumor which accounted for his recent loss of energy and weight. Surgery was his only recourse.

This gentle man listened to my evaluation. With a short, sideways glance at his son who nodded affirmation, Billy bravely told me to make arrangements. He had too much to do to let this event hold him down.

Insurance company life expectancy tables do not go as high as 99 years. Imagine the premiums! I looked at the person instead of the statistics and found a man with a large amount of life left. Billy was very much alive, in general good health, very active, and in a close, loving family. His lively mind and optimistic outlook went well with his warm personality and keen sense of humor. Yes, I thought, Billy needed and deserved this chance.

A few days later, I held Billy's hand as he went to sleep on the operating table. His thin, gray hair, covered with a paper cap, made him look comical. Billy had seen the humor in his getup as well and mentioned it as we moved him onto the table. There was peace in his hazel eyes. His body appeared much more frail now stripped of his baggy clothing, but he was relaxed and obviously comfortable with whatever would come. I held his hand and he drifted to sleep.

———◆———

There are times in the operating room when I feel a Power guiding my actions. I become the instrument rather than the prime mover. I experience the "channel" of healing Francis of Assisi spoke about. Am I the actor, or am I being acted upon? It is a wonderful feeling and reminds me that surgery can be a holy thing. This is how I felt during Billy's operation, and I allowed myself to go with it.

The surgery was over in just under an hour. Recovery was unbelievably smooth and uncomplicated. Three days later, I walked into his room and mentally played "Circle What's Wrong with This Picture." This centenarian sat up in bed placidly contemplating the beeping IVAC pump on his IV hookup. A nasogastric tube was taped to his nose and connected to the wall suction where it kept his stomach empty of its content. On the table sat a partially eaten Italian sandwich.

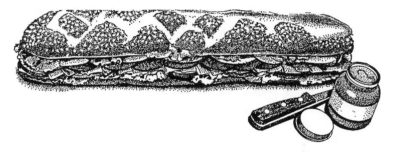

I demanded with agitation to know whose hoagie this was. "Mine," Billy answered. "Why are you eating a submarine sandwich! Who gave it to you?" I bellowed. "I'd rather not say," Billy calmly responded. I was beside myself thinking all my beautiful stitches would burst with this most unorthodox first, post op meal. Then he tacked on, "I was hungry." Indeed!

By the fifth post op day when most people start to sip liquids and struggle out of bed, Billy strolled the ward — cane in hand, a student nurse on each arm! While Billy did need the cane, it was apparent that the student nurses were pure icing. Realizing there was nothing more we could do for him, I discharged Billy.

In three not six weeks, Billy was back in full action. This 99-

year old man recovered in half the time it takes younger patients. So much for usual and customary!

If statistics could not explain Billy, perhaps he could. I could not wait to sit him down for a talk. I knew a few things about Billy from his friends and relatives. This wonderful, personable man loved his family. He loved fishing almost as much and would grin sagely when asked about fishing holes or the right bait. "Billy, tell me the secret of a long, meaningful life," I asked during his follow-up exam. He pulled up his trousers and snapped the suspenders over his shoulders. I was talking to a cross between St. Thomas Aquinas and Bob Hope.

"Three things to remember," he began. "First, it's important to go fishing every day. If possible, eat what you catch," he waved one finger in the air. "You know, God does not count against you the days that you fish. So I'm really only 18!" I chuckled, my attention undivided.

"Second," another finger was extended, "always have both short and long term goals. Do something you *have* to do, and also something you *like*. But, don't have too many goals 'cause you'll never feel like you get anything done." I asked him what one of his goals might be. "To get my name announced by the fat man on the *Today* show when I turn 100. . . . What's his name? . . . Oh yeah, Willard Scott!"

"Finally, the most important thing of all," three fingers were now before my expectant face. "Surround yourself with people who keep their minds full and their bowels empty. But it seems to me that most people do exactly the opposite." I laughed heartily and thought about all the people with empty minds and full bowels that I should start eliminating immediately from my life!

Billy laughed as he laid it out. At his age, he had been asked the same question lots of times and had experienced plenty of opportunity to sharpen his thoughts. He mused about how hard it was for young people to accept his notions. The answers are simple, but easier said than done.

At its most basic level, Billy's philosophy requires an understanding and acceptance of who and what we are. That is something that most people struggle with — or against — most of their lives. Life never turns out to be all we hoped it would. My mother used to say that God got it all backwards. We should all be born at 80 and grow younger, smarter and healthier with time.

We are never as strong, smart, good looking, lucky or successful as we thought we would be . . . or as other people seem to be. If we allow ourselves to be consumed by the disappointment of inevitable failures, we never enjoy what we do achieve.

Billy, on the other hand, made the best of what he had been given. Instead of seeing life in terms of limitations and frustrations, he actively sought and found opportunities. He accomplished and enjoyed new challenges every day.

Fish every day. Eat what you catch. Fishing was Billy's fun. But it could also put food on the table and provide healthful benefits of fresh air and exercise. All gain, no pain. Not a bad deal!

Wake up with something to do. Have a reason to get up, get dressed, get breakfast and get moving. No time to sit about feeling sorry for yourself. No need to check every ache and pain. Get up with a project in mind and get it done first thing. Once done, the day is a success. Something worthwhile is accomplished and the rest of the day is gravy.

Have goals — but not too many. We are our own worst critics. We please ourselves the least. We all know people who are busy with so many projects they can not possibly get them all done. Others accomplish astonishing goals in one day, but they are never satisfied. Evening approaches with them strung up, worn out and frustrated, dreading the morning alarm clock.

In our fast-paced society, it is easy, even encouraged, to get caught up in that rat race. The single-minded, type-A's are rewarded for countless hours spent on the job to the exclusion of everything else. That kind of drive is hard to sustain year after year, and it exacts its price in burnout, health problems, and often times sorrow. No matter how much we achieve, nobody ever looks back and wishes he had spent more time at the office.

When Billy says to have goals but not too many, he means to be realistic. It is one thing to know what you want out of life. But it is much more important to know the price you are willing to pay. Otherwise, you will never know until it is too late whether what you are getting is worth what you are giving up.

Surround yourself with people who keep their minds full and their bowels empty! Speaking of dull! People who are the other way around drag you down. They see no wonder in life. They have no enthusiasm to share and see only the downside, the reasons for <u>not</u> doing things. Fearing failure, they avoid involvement. Billy's imagery is right on the mark. Empty minds, full bowels — the feeling it evokes is of a painful need for a catharsis. Black clouded people smother every spark of brightness and enthusiasm only if we let them.

One unfortunate aspect of getting older is that for too many people, age brings bitterness. Those inclined toward joy and vitality should seek kindred spirits, people determined not to grow old with resentment, anger and disappointment.

I've had plenty of reasons to stay in touch with Billy and his family. I have since operated on his son, granddaughter, and great-grandson. Billy has been back frequently for follow-up visits. When he turned 100, my whole staff stood out in the hall and sang *Happy Birthday* to him.

Billy, a few weeks short of 103, recently died at the end of a short illness. He remained cancer free, full of life and love, a pleasure to be around. His funeral service was a celebration of his life not a mourning of his death. I will miss him, but will always hold the gift of his example to me as a lifelong treasure.

As I mentioned, it was my privilege to grow up in an Italian neighborhood in South Philly in a close, extended family. My Gram' Mary had two kitchens, one in the basement and one upstairs — doesn't everyone? She loved to cook. Eating food was one of life's opportunities to celebrate with others. In the basement, she rolled homemade pasta on an old wood board, polished with all the flour and spaghetti that had passed over it. In later years, I suspected we lived with Gram' because we were less affluent than most. But who could ever feel poor in the midst of all that love and food. I thought I was the richest, luckiest kid on earth. And I was.

The two most important women in my early life, Gram' Mary and Mom, were clean freaks. Sweep! Dust! Polish! — even the marble steps on the front stoop, the sidewalk, and the curb! My father would tease, "Never know when the Queen of England is going to stop by."

Those were the days before triple track, hinged windows, but never would there be even a dried raindrop on Gram's windows. Winter, summer, no matter, each window was washed inside and out. Armed with cleaning rags and a blue bottle of Windex, these two wonders would shimmy out on the narrow ledges, reach up and scrub away until each pane was shiny and spotless.

One day before I'd even started to school, I glanced up from my bouncing ball on the sidewalk and saw Gram' Mary hanging out the third floor attacking windows with Sicilian zeal. Her foot swung over the sill as her skirt billowed in the wind.

Terror seized my heart. The fragility of her circumstance frightened me. It was the first inkling of mortality I can remember. I saw her and the hard cement three stories below. I panicked!

Flying into the house and up the steps to the third floor bedroom,

I screamed at her, "What's the matter with you!? Don't you know you could fall and die?" And then I said something that I was made never to forget for the rest of my life. "You're too old for that," I blurted.

Gram' did not mince words or beat around bushes. She came right to the point, "You shud-uppa you face," she screamed. "I like-a doing this. I like-a my house clean. I don't ever wanna anyone to say I'm dirty. Don't you ever tella me I'm too old to do something again. Old is when you stop doing the things you love."

Something like that, you never forget. It was still strong in my memory years later, when Gram' broke her hip. By then, she lived alone in her house but her zest for life had not diminished. That day she had been in the basement cooking. When she tried to carry the heavy, wooden board laden with fresh pasta, she fell. She lay at the bottom of the steps nearly a full day and night before her cries of pain aroused the worried neighbors. They hadn't seen her out with her broom or making her daily round of errands. Six weeks later, she died of heart failure. Those last days were the only time I saw her ill. Even then she remained strong willed and feisty.

She was my mentor. Her greatest pleasure was doing for others. She was a fiscal fool and gave away more than she made. But she was loved and appreciated for her good heart and fierce independence. She was not beholden to anyone and certainly was never a burden.

Did she decide that her time was up? Did she will her death? I have often wondered. To tell the truth, I would not be surprised if she did call her last shot. Nor would anyone who has spent any time caring for older people. You see it in their eyes. They are tired, worn out, and do not want to go on anymore.

In Gram Mary's case, her will to live took her to a ripe, old age. She had a good life with no regrets. Facing maybe the rest of her life bedridden or in a wheelchair and dependent on others to keep her clean, she may have given up. Who's to tell her she had to keep fighting to maintain a life that may have lost all meaning and dignity for her? Not me.

What worries me are those who give up the fight before it is ever begun, those who surrender before the battle is waged.

Take my friend, Louie, a retiree who had recently lost to cancer his wife, best friend, and lifelong companion. They had been inseparable. It was a marriage that others would envy and emulate. Throughout his wife's final days, Louie had been hospice nurse, faithful partner, loving confidant.

When she at last found peace, he was devastated. He had never imagined life without her. Alone, empty, he was inconsolable.

A year and a half later, suffering from severe weight loss and anemia, he came to my office. When I told him the diagnosis, a large bowel cancer, his reaction stunned me. Instead of being dismayed by the bad news, he was elated. He wished with all his heart for his life to end. I had just handed him a non-Kevorkian solution to his dilemma.

In his case, I did scream, a little anyway. I tried to change the direction of his thinking. It worked well enough to get Louie to agree to counseling. What emerged from deep within was an entirely normal, healthy fear of dying. Hope also glimmered. Maybe there was something more in life he needed to do.

Louie eventually agreed to major surgery, radiation and chemo-therapy. After his successful treatment, he joined a senior citizens group where he met a beautiful Italian lady (of course!), Bella. For the first time in his life, he found himself on a dance floor. Soon he started doing other things he had not done before. His new lady got him to sing in the church choir. He found a penchant for poetry to release his feelings of loss. Louie surprised himself with his ability to be articulate and expressive. Bella taught him the wonders of Italian food. He discovered that garlic did not necessarily give one gas and that red wine and hot peppers go well with lots of foods.

Three years after agreeing to surgery, Louie still misses his wife. But instead of wanting to die, he is glad he decided to embrace life. He knows now what everybody who wants a long life learns — life goes on with or without you. Life is an individual experience that is not over until we decide it is.

Billy, Gram', Louie — so much of what I know about life I have taken from the wisdom of older people.

Go fishing, eat what you catch. Have goals each day-but not too many. Surround yourself with knowledgeable people who don't walk around your clean mind with their dirty shoes. Still, the most important words of wisdom I ever got were the ones handed to me by Gram' Mary years ago.

"Shud-uppa you face" and listen to what others are saying. That last part was added by me — but only after I wised up to what she really meant.

Touchstones

What is the most frequently played, negative message in your mind? Give yourself a good argument against it.

Risky Business

You can't wait for all the traffic lights to turn
green before you start driving across town.
Ernie Miller

Sometimes, there is no comfortable way out of a predicament.

I agreed to say a few words at a gathering of cancer survivors. It seemed like a good idea. However, when the time came, I was literally left standing in the dark in the middle of a football stadium.

The only light came from a double row of luminaries, paper bags glowing with candlelight, which coursed around the running track. Scores more flickered a dramatic backdrop in the stands. In the darkness, the glow of all these candles spelled out the evening's message:

Cancer survivors, friends and families were in the midst of a *Relay for Life*. As part of a nationwide effort to remember the brave victims, both living and dead, the local cancer society was conducting a 24-hour event. Its purpose was to raise money from sponsors who would support teams as they did laps around the track.

I felt honored just being there. It was difficult to know precisely what to say to be inspirational. Heck, the inspiration was flowing the other way! As the lights dimmed, I thought about some of the remarks I had put together. Suddenly struck by the scene around me, I canned my prepared talk.

I spoke of my friend, Mac, who comes as close to an honest-to-gosh hero as anyone I know. He spent 20 years as a Marine, including two combat tours in Vietnam and another dangerous tour in the Middle East. Standing six foot six, there was little I feared in his company. Groups of people literally parted for him. He was the Marine right off a recruiting poster.

Mac had a childhood that might have ruined a lesser person. He did not grow up with many viable options. The Marines may have been the best way out of a tough home life, and he used the experience to make the best of himself.

I met him through my wife. Joyce and her best friend, Peggy, were inseparable through high school and college. They roomed together during their graduate training in Cincinnati. Mac, then in South Carolina, would hitchhike several hundred miles on Friday night to salvage a small part of the weekend with Peggy. Often he would sleep in bath tubs or storage stalls to avoid night checks that often took place in the girls' dorm. Those were the days when rules about male visitors were strictly enforced.

Mac married Peggy when she finished her schooling and immediately was off on his first Southeast Asia tour. I met Joyce about the same time. We happened to be married as Mac was returning and we four became fast friends.

When Mac had put in his 20 years, he and Peggy settled a few miles from us. Still young, with a solid background in people management and a suitable personality to boot, he made friends and gained respect easily. It looked like hard times were over.

It was a terrible shock to all of us when, at the age of 46, he was diagnosed with leukemia. That is about as grim as it can get. His kind of disease typically carried a poor prognosis. Death, he was told, would be painfully swift. It was hardly fair — to everyone except this remarkable human being.

Most of us, myself included, might have cursed and raged, expending energy too precious to waste. We might have pronounced life's fortunes diabolic and quickly succumbed to our fate. Mac recognized that life is difficult. Truer words were never spoken. As a matter of fact, they are the first three words of a very famous book by Scott Peck entitled *The Road Less Traveled.*

Mac spent energy in positive directions. He feverishly researched all options — even those most experts labeled dangerous or "exceedingly nontraditional." The one that promised the best chance at longevity also brought the most suffering. It was the one that guaranteed the greatest inconvenience and the one most likely to hasten his death if unsuccessful. "Never tell me the odds," he joked as he chose a bone marrow transplant.

In theory, it sounds simple. Kill off all the diseased bone marrow with high dose chemotherapy and replace it with healthy tissue from a suitably matched donor. The leukemia will be gone and the donor marrow will guarantee normal immune function.

In practice, though, drug therapy can create agonizing side effects: nausea, mouth sores, gastrointestinal complications, hair loss, and delirium.

A compatible donor is difficult to find. The body's normal reaction to the transplant must be suppressed with anti-rejection medicine, with the unavoidable side effect of increased infection. Then there is something called Graft Versus Host disease, a terrible problem in which the graft of bone marrow actually rejects the patient, killing him painfully in the process. Finally, the patient may get to the point where the transplant simply won't work and then the patient dies defenseless from lack of immunity.

Mac found four compatible donors. Unheard of! He spent several weeks undergoing what became a lifesaving procedure. This hulk of a man was reduced to something snipers' bullets and months of armed conflict never approached. He lost 80 pounds, battled delirium, and suffered much.

One year has passed. The sores and pain are mostly gone. We spent one night celebrating with him at our house. My wife baked a cake with a single glowing candle to celebrate Mac's first haircut in a year. He now has a future because he was willing to fight for the long odds and put himself to the test.

Understandably, Mac is extremely grateful to his donor. *Thank yous* must wait because there is a waiting period before donor and recipient can, if they chose, learn each others' identities. The delay is intended to protect the donor from the grief should the donated marrow be rejected and the recipient die.

Mac did not wait to begin paying back. He volunteered as a Big Brother, to help a boy whose life is just as difficult as his own once was. At least for now, his story has a happy ending.

As I stood in that flickering light, I realized that this story was not necessarily one you would want to stress to a stadium packed with people facing their own imminent demise or for others grieving the dead.

Odds are getting better, but cases of cancer like Mac's that end in a cure remain the exception. It would be cruel, discouraging and not at all inspirational to throw a happy ending into the faces of people who know this.

So what I emphasized as I told Mac's story was his willingness to fight. A brave man looked inside and saw fear. Anyone who has not been fearful, particularly under these circumstances, is not courageous. Lack of fear is not bravery or courage. It is some kind of insanity! It is okay to be afraid! What saved him from his fear is what saves each of us from ours — the willingness to accept the risk it takes to overcome it.

Whether on the battlefield staring down an enemy's muzzle or on the oncology ward, carrying a dreaded enemy within, fear dominates.

From birth on, risk is an unavoidable part of life. There is no surefire, painless, risk-free path through this world. We all weigh options and take chances. There's a poem called "Advice From Debbie" that states: "Make your decision and then forget about it . . . the moment of absolute certainty never comes."

It is no easier for those who have fought battles before. When the cup is passed to them, their reaction is the same: "Why me, Lord?"

Relax, it is not as bleak as it might seem. All things are relative. One of my favorite lecturers and writers is Leo Buscaglia, not necessarily because we share the same first name and Italian heritage, but because Buscaglia isn't afraid to face up to life, love and feeling.

Once I was privileged to hear him say something that reaches to the heart of what we have been talking about. "I would rather feel pain than feel nothing at all." Existential touching, feeling and hugging serve me notice of my existence. They tell me I am alive. Much can be learned from feelings, even pain.

There is no choice. Pain, if nothing else is an affirmation of life. Stick a pin into an injured limb, and if it jumps in pain, it is still alive. It is still capable of feeling. The absence of pain is not good. It portends destruction, uselessness and death.

Another of my favorite writers is that prolific, eternal, Greek philosopher and poet, Anonymous. Old Anon is credited with penning a poem titled "Risk" (which I include in its entirety at the back of this chapter). The author artfully argues that risk is a two-edged sword because not taking risks poses its own risks.

"To try," the poet says, "risks failure," but "the greatest hazard in life is to risk nothing. The person who risks nothing does nothing, has nothing, and is nothing. He may avoid suffering and sorrow, but he cannot learn, feel, change, grow, love and live."

Our unknown wise man goes on to conclude that the person who avoids risk "has forfeited his freedom. Only a person who risks," he insists, "is truly free."

However, one who risks is not totally free. Not free to be reckless and foolhardy. There is enormous wiggle room separating <u>no</u> risk from <u>all</u> risk. The degree of risk is something that has to be carefully calculated and weighed against potential benefits.

You put your hand on the hot stove only once when you are a child to realize there is not much point in doing that again. Even folks who engage in potentially hazardous activities, like jumping out of airplanes, always check their parachutes first.

There are things each person has to decide for himself. Mac made his choice in accepting a high degree of risk and pain for a small chance at living. Not everyone would feel comfortable with his choice, nor should they. Choices, like people, are unique and individual.

———— • ————

When I think of Mac on the one hand, my mind usually drifts to Bill on the other. My involvement with Bill goes back many years to when he and his wife first started coming to our cancer support sessions.

Bill had incurable kidney cancer, and it had spread to his lung. He was traveling 60 miles to Philadelphia for chemotherapy. It was not working. Worse, the chemicals made him feel so sick that life hardly seemed worth living. Bill, a professional man with great intelligence and insight, was also a very spiritual person. He and his wife, despite his problems, gave much more to the group than they could ever hope to get in return. What they had to face was not an easy decision.

Chemotherapy was the only measure of hope Bill's doctors could offer. But, after lengthy discussions and a great deal of soul searching, the couple reached a comfortable decision. They would stop the chemo. Bill's doctors did not object. They agreed he'd be better off and better able to enjoy what life remained.

Life is full of unexplained turns. Who knows why, but Bill's body found the resources needed to rebound. His tumors began shrinking, and within several months they were practically gone.

For months, Bill lived in a symbiosis with his tumor, able to enjoy life more fully. Though ultimately his cancer has returned, a number of new and promising therapies loom on the horizon to treat its recurrence.

While Bill and Mac made different choices for different reasons, both accepted the inevitability of risk. In hindsight, it is clear they both made the right choice, but hindsight is always 20-20. Those who make choices that do not turn out this well are no less successful. The ultimate resolution comes in becoming whole, healing. The decision affects a healing even if a cure does not ensue. Those who died with their risks in control were heroes and brave, too. Only the indecisive were left behind.

In this modern, antiseptic, air-conditioned world, we are tempted to think we can control all the variables. It just is not possible. The universe, God, Fate . . . whatever you call the Creative Life Force that nurtures and sustains, has a plan for us. Sometimes the choices we make and the risks we take help fulfill that plan. Sometimes, they go against it. Our attempts at control are pretensions that make the wise howl in derision.

———— ◆ ————

A man of the soil plants his seed corn not ever knowing how much rain the season will bring. He can not determine his yield or what the market will pay. There are good and bad years, some-

times coming in bunches. Yet, each spring farmers with new optimism plow, plant and take their chances.

There is a man in our county who knew the farmer's way. A farmer and dairyman, he

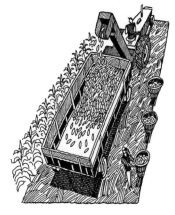

got himself elected to political office. Ernie often found himself on the outs with city slicker politicians. They were loath to take risks with public money or popular opinion until all the risks had been wrung out of the proposition. This was, according to Ernie, a surefire formula for doing nothing.

Once, in total exasperation of all the pronouncers of nervous negativism, Ernie put it as plainly as it has ever been said: "You can't wait for all the lights to turn green," he argued with impeccable logic, " before you start driving across town."

Indeed, you can not.

Risks

To laugh is to risk appearing the fool.
To weep is to risk appearing sentimental.
To reach out to another is to risk involvement.
To expose feeling is to risk exposing your true self.
To place your ideas, your dreams before a crowd
*   is to risk their loss.*
To love is to risk not being loved in return.
To live is to risk dying.
To hope is to risk despair.
To try is to risk failure.
But risks must be taken because the greatest hazard
*   in life is to risk nothing.*
The person who risks nothing, does nothing, has
*   nothing and is nothing.*
He may avoid suffering and sorrow, but he cannot
*   learn, feel, change, grow, love and live.*
Chained by his certitudes, he is a slave.
He has forfeited his freedom.
Only the person who risks is truly free.

Anonymous

Wellsprings

Emily: "Oh, earth, you're too wonderful
for anybody to realize you. ... Do any
human beings ever realize life while
they live it? — every, every minute?"

Thornton Wilder, *Our Town*

Healing before Curing

It's all right. You don't have to fight anymore.
You've done your best. It's all right to let go.
My surgical mentor to an elderly patient at the
moment of her death, many years ago

Self-help books are everywhere. One large source is from the so-called *New Age Movement* which challenges us to take ownership of our health. By forcing awareness and intelligently exploring options, New Agers have prodded all to examine health and lifestyle choices.

Smoking. Cholesterol. Diets. Massage. Acupuncture. Imaging. Meditation. These and other topics are discussed as prophylactic means to healthy ends. Books. Seminars. Counseling. Videos. Pathways to attaining new knowledge are endless. This book, *Touchstones and Wellsprings*, discusses ideas from my point of view, but, let's get one thing straight. This text should not be labeled "New Age." It is not.

Labels lock in, close out, confuse and have a way of turning people off, including me. Principles discussed here concern healing in its rudimentary and primary form. Healing. Not curing. There is a vast difference. While there are lots of books on getting well, staying well, and curing ills, the list of good texts on healing is short.

Bernie Siegel's works along with an excellent piece by Larry Dossey come to mind immediately. There are others. These books and this chapter in particular will discuss *healing* in a general, basic way.

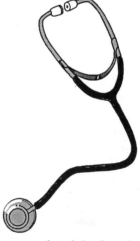

It was one of those days. As a surgical resident at the Hospital of the University of Pennsylvania, I had a wall full of certificates to prove I was a doctor. But, what gives meaning to being a doctor cannot be neatly lettered in calligraphy, framed in oak, and hung on a wall.

I had worked days with an elderly woman in the final stages of malignancy. I had poured over her charts, done research, checked diagnostic tests, examined her frail body — everything my years of learning had taught me to make her comfortable.

But all I did was annoy her. No smile. No eye contact. No "thank you." Her lack of gratitude added to my fatigue and frustration. I was grateful to make rounds with her surgeon, also my instructor, an upbeat fellow who put a positive spin on even the worst of days. I needed his encouragement with this patient.

When we arrived in her room, I decorously picked up her chart and began presenting her problems to update him. I fished for a pat-on-the-back, a doctor-to-doctor pick-me-up.

My mentor ignored me, paying not the least attention to my droning. Instead, he did something I had never seen another surgeon do and certainly had not read in any text book. He sat on the edge of her bed, breaking through the professional barrier. As he brushed matted, gray hair from her forehead, he gently touched her waxen face with the back of his hand then kissed her tenderly on the cheek. He picked up her pale, emaciated hand and placed it in his!

I was rendered speechless as I witnessed the essence of greatness in medicine. Humbly, I stepped back and observed, silently praying, "Lord, help me learn."

The dying woman smiled warmly at this man. In my eyes, he loomed larger than I had ever imagined. His firm, reassuring voice said, "It's all right. You don't have to fight anymore, Madeline. You've done your best. It's all right to let go."

She smiled at his words. Tension visibly drained from her body. She sighed deeply, relaxed, and closed her eyes. In a moment, that was all. Steadfastly, he held her hand and looked into her trusting eyes.

It was the first time I had been present at the moment of death. Oh, I had been at resuscitations and cardiac arrests and other moments of panic or crisis. I had even pronounced patients *officially dead*. But I had never before been present at the exact moment when a human being gently just lets go.

It seemed so natural. Sacred. My mentor unashamedly wiped tears from his eyes. Consumed with overwhelming jealousy and envy, I was nowhere near the healer this man was.

At last, he turned to me to answer the raging sea of emotional questions which silently poured from my heart. His tale was simple. He loved this old woman. He felt deeply for her as he helped her the past few months and her personhood grew for him. Like everyone who has walked this earth, she had run in the rain, felt joy at the birth of her children, toted troubles, and shared sorrows. Physicians are often privileged, if they are open, to experience the synapse and sanctity of one human being touching another.

When they had gone as far as they could in treating her disease, he had given her the last measure of healing he possessed — the permission to die.

I recalled his gentle way of finding something to touch the souls of frightened patients with all kinds of horrible illnesses. He touched my soul, too. With a hug that symbolized unity of purpose, he reassured these people, "I'll do my best for you."

As we walked several floors from Madeline's room, my mind was still a jumble. He turned the page to another chapter of wisdom from *Physicianship Excellence.* It would take me years to fully comprehend. *Never, ever forget the difference between curing and healing.*

That night underscored the distinction between doctor and physician.

I love it when my friend, the bestselling writer and lecturer Bernie Siegel, asks an audience if there is anyone who was not lovable when they were a minute old. A few times I've seen people raise hands. Their self esteem was so beaten down, they can not even imagine themselves loved as a newborn!

This deprecation is sad because it is so untrue. Except for the worst, most evil, most misanthropic sociopaths, we are hard-wired to love little babies. The survival of our species depends upon it.

So, at least for that first minute of life, we are all lovable. All. It is our inheritance, as writer and psychiatrist Jerry Jampolsky says. God and parents give love that becomes our dowry. And at that moment of birth, each one of us reflects love.

If we can accept that fact even grudgingly, as Bernie argues to his audiences, then we are faced with an astounding proposition. To accept love as our inheritance is a right of birth. To love and be loved are our only birthrights.

Then comes those other hundreds of thousands of minutes after that first hopeful, pristine, promising one. We begin to fill up with "stuff." "Stuff " can be symphonies and praise, rainbows and knowledge, benchmarks and baggage. It is put there by many people: parents, teachers, relatives, friends, strangers. Some enlighten and enrich, while others demean, insult and denigrate.

"Don't you know what 'no' means? Can't you sit still like other good kids? Why must you always go out of your way to get yourself in trouble? Why can't you behave the way you're supposed to? You are so stupid!"

Yes, too many children have had an earful of negativism. Home and school aren't the worst of it. Other kids can be cruel, too.

"Four eyes. Pizza face. Fatty. Jerk. Nerd. Loser."

Know what? It becomes a way of life, a vicious circle. Those abused and scorned learn this destructive behavior. Their Life templates become contaminated and warped. Sadly, they often turn around and abuse others. They follow the old pecking order.

Children are born with a natural inclination to trust. They believe what they hear. "I love you." — said in words or by deed — wraps gently around their psyche and provides a fulcrum for their lives. Conversely, messages of derision and hate are as corrosive as battery acid. Mentally, we play the messages we are given over and over. Good or bad, we believe. The mind is a powerful force.

Imprinting is not something which ends in childhood. Our psyche and ego are ravenous and fragile. We all need stamped, *"Handle with care!"* Important interactions and messages come from spouses, children, co-workers, friends, teachers, and the guy in a brown jumpsuit delivering packages.

Anyone can make (or break!) our day.

Have we permitted our birthright, our precious inheritance of love to be shoved aside? Have we let negative critters inside to create self-doubt, insecurity, indecisiveness, intolerance, fear, anger and resentment? The last is probably the biggest negative baggage of all and more than enough negative force to pull anyone under.

A Jesuit friend of mine told me that the greatest sin is not murder, adultery, theft or any of the other traditional evils. It is the fear to become one's self, the wonderful *me* that was determined by my genes to become a unique human being.

Instead, many of us follow a vicious downward spiral. Siegel and others teach us that the only way to break out is through a bridge called *forgiveness*, the root of great religions and pyschotherapies. If we are burdened by self flagellation, guilt and shame, the bridge we build to our inheritance, can only be traversed by first and foremost forgiving ourselves.

Ease up! When we are not so hard on ourselves, an incredible thing happens. The moment we feel self forgiveness, we start on the path to *true* humility not head-down, breast-beaten and wimpish humility. Not at all. Rather, we achieve the ability to love and accept who we are — faults, past digressions, imperfections, and even fat thighs. Go look in the mirror. Go ahead, now! See goodness. It is there. Love and forgive that wonderful person who looks back at you.

Now you have made an essential start to wholeness and peace.

The next step is forgiveness of others. Hey, others possess faults just like us! Often we tear people down or build them up for all the wrong reasons. Usually we tear someone down because we have had a rotten day. "You stupid jerk!" we wave our fist out the window. "Why don't you learn how to drive!" We have dehumanized that other driver. We would never have the nerve to yell such balderdash to their face. We drive off down the road, fuming but anonymous.

We tear our children down with condemnation instead of trying to open dialogue. "How could you have missed that basket! What's the matter? Do you have two left feet!" We should say, "You played a hard game. I'll bet you were disappointed it didn't turn out differently."

Framing is everything.
Examine how you look at things. Examine how you say things. Examine the messages you play in your mind day after day.

As I mentioned, we also sometimes build people up for the wrong reasons. Jane is married to a kind man, but he lacks ambition and outside interests. Money and excitement are often missing in their marriage. Instead of focusing on her husband's good traits and helping him grow, Jane uses her best friend's husband as an index of what is *normal*. "Sue and Paul have the perfect marriage. He has a good job. They take trips and are always going to parties. Why am I married to such a loser!"

The truth of the matter is, if we all took our problems and heartaches, put them in a bag, then lined up with them and told you to choose one, you would probably pick your own lot. We are all cut from the same cloth. Become a deft tailor and create a life garment of wonder and beauty. Love first yourself. Then you can love others.

A bumper sticker proclaims, "God don't make no junk!" If we think *we* are junk or that *others* are junk, and if God did not make it, then who did? We did, of course.

Why is this so important to me? I'm a surgeon, not a psychiatrist.

I will tell you why. Sarah walked into my office. I sat her down and we discussed her test results. She had cancer and needed radical, disfiguring surgery, radiation therapy and chemotherapy. If we got it all, she might survive.

Shoulders slumped, head down, eyes focused on an invisible point in the middle of my desk, Sarah groaned low and pitifully.

After decades of guiding patients through similar scenarios, I have a good feel for the mettle depth of each individual. Sometimes my patients surprise me, but I could tell Sarah did not hold out much hope for anything but tragedy. She had been beaten down I found out later. Slashed by an unhappy marriage and contentious divorce, and raped by financial difficulties that left her and the children submerged in a sea of debt, she seemed to take bitter satisfaction from every piece of bad news that I lay on her.

Now, I can help *cure* her cancer, but can I *heal* the patient? In her present condition, I am afraid not. I know from past experience, even if I can excise every cancer cell from her body, it will only be a matter of time until there is another medical hurdle.

So, we talk for an hour, not about medicine but about her. I need to show Sarah that I — another human being! — care. If she accepts my caring, then she is on the road to seeing that others care, too. I want to get her into a support group. If . . . if . . . if.

Then maybe she can be more than *cured*; she can be *healed*.

———— • ————

Am I hoping for miracles? No, not at all. I do not believe in the traditional view of Biblical miracles. John Taylor, in *Notes on an Unhurried Journey* provides an interesting twist on the subject.

Most of us, he says, try to bargain with God when we face difficult problems. Just take this away and I will promise anything. Just get me off the hook. But what if, Taylor asks, the world abounded in miracles? What if, at the snap of our fingers, we could escape random fate and avoid dire consequences?

What need would we have for each other? We could live our lives in total isolation with no care or concern for anyone else. Then what meaning would life have?

Instead of foolishly praying for miracles, we should be hoping to be graced by another word. Mercy. Mercy is as easily attainable as one person reaching out to another in time of need. Yet from a distance, Taylor says, "It is hard to tell mercy apart from miracle, and maybe that is miracle enough."

As I write this chapter, our nation is reeling from a terrorist attack on Oklahoma City. A bomb blast caused devastating loss of life, yet in the midst of horror, even as bodies were being counted, a remarkable thing was unfolding. Even as a grieving community sought reasons *Why!?*, a miracle happened.

People began reaching out to each other, not just victims' families clinging together to share the burden of their losses, but everyone. Perfect strangers, seeing pain in each others' eyes, stopped for hugs, perhaps for the first time. There was no end to the help that was freely given to the sufferers and the rescuers.

It was not just Oklahoma City. It changed us all. It made us very aware of the various conflicts that have divided us. Maybe we had turned too much away from each other. The thought crossed more than a few minds that maybe we ought to turn back before it is too late. I have no explanation for the sickness that compels misdirected minds to commit such acts. I offer no answer. But, I contend that it is a miracle that so much good should come from so much evil. Or is it mercy? As Taylor says, you can not really tell.

———◆———

One of the most profound miracles recorded in the New Testament is Jesus' raising Lazarus from the dead. For what? To die again? This miracle always has troubled me. No disrespect meant, but we all are going to die. No one gets out of this world alive. In the raising of Lazarus, I find a great conflict that spills over into the practice of medicine.

Physicians are trained to take every heroic measure within reason to extend life. We are also taught to regard death in many ways as a *failure*. The implication is always there. Life equals success. Death equals failure. My profession has difficulty even saying the "D" word. So we say *passing, leaving* or *expired*. We just cannot bring ourselves to say the word *death*.

Yes, everyone dies. What meandering, contorted path must our conversations with our patients take then?

———— • ————

Recently, I found myself in the hospital room of an old friend I will call June. Years before, I had helped save her life by repairing a rupturing abdominal aortic aneurysm. June moved away and I did not see her until she came back to console her daughter whose husband was terminally ill. Tragically, on the day he died, June's daughter died of a heart attack. No one will ever convince me it was not a broken heart. Theirs was the only double funeral I ever witnessed. I remember the matching caskets placed head to head.

Now June was hospitalized again with lung cancer. She was frail and in pain with labored breathing. Without thinking, I sat on the edge of the bed. For a long time, I remained there, silent with tears in my eyes. She woke and smiled weakly. I did not know what to say, so I said nothing.

June finally spoke. She said she was afraid to die. I asked why. "I don't want to be alone," she barely whispered. I looked into her eyes to the depth of her soul and assured her, "You are not alone." She smiled again, squeezed my hand and was gone. No big fanfare. Just healing. I left her room. We were both at peace.

———— • ————

There is a young medical student, a great kid named Rob. He gently ribs me and says he wants to grow up just like me. I tell him fat and bald is a heck of a way to go through life.

It is a funny thing. I watch him relate to patients, see his warmth and patience. I witness his love, and I can see myself in him. And I can see my old professor in me. It is a profound harvest when fertile seeds of love, nurturing and caring can be sown through generations.

What would I want the next generation of doctors to know? That there is nothing wrong with being there when people die? Yes, for sure. That it is the priestly role of the healer to give people permission to do what they must when they face death?

Mostly I want him to know that in letting go, it is in no way a defeat or failure. These folks are not throwing hands up in surrender. They are reaching out for the gift of their final healing.

Their immortality.

 Wellsprings

Lord make me an instrument of Your peace. Where there is hatred let me sow love; where there is injury, pardon; where there is doubt, faith; where there is despair, hope; where there is darkness, light; and where there is sadness, joy. O divine master, grant that I may not so much seek to be consoled as to console; to be understood as to understand; to be loved as to love. For it is in giving that we receive; it is in pardoning that we are pardoned; and it is in dying that we are born to eternal life.   Francis of Assisi

Choice Pickings

There is no living and there is no dying.
You are either alive, or you're dead.
Donna, the big sister of S.E.E.K., support group for "incurables"

I am an incurable romantic.   Let Cupid's arrows fly.   Let D.W.Griffith direct plots for my life.   Let John Williams write my sound tracks.   I will stand tall, stay strong and keep the faith. In the end, I will kiss the heroine and slay dragons as the screen fades to black. . . . In all my dreams, perhaps.

The truth is, I face the same realities as everyone. If Hollywood filmed my life story, Redford or Newman would not play the lead as I fantasize. Something tells me The Keystone Cops, Little Rascals, or the crew from Saturday Night Live would be closer to the real thing.

Take that day on the beach a few years ago. Waves broke fifty feet away under an azure sky. Cotton clouds had the Good House-keeping Stamp of Approval. Gulls dipped into a shoreline caressed by a cool breeze. I lounged with a book in my corner of paradise, when out of nowhere strolls a beautiful, Botticellian lady clad in a skimpy bikini. She stopped square in front of me and stared!

"You old dog!" I said to myself. "You haven't lost it yet. Wait till I tell my wife!"

I intoned with all the suave I could muster and a smile far too broad, "Can I help you?" I sucked in my breath, increasing my thorax and decreasing my abdominal cavity, a primal reflex probably practiced by middle-aged, grunting cavemen. I hoped I would not have to hold this Atlas pose too long, but I didn't want this ego trip to end.

After a pause, she cooed, "Boy, you must be depressed. Can I help?"

I exhaled explosively. My abdomen flopped to its natural anatomic position. "No, no," I stammered. "I'm really okay. Jeez, thanks though for asking . . . I guess." I smiled weakly wondering what the hell she was talking about.

She walked away, shaking her head. I sank back into my chair and reality sank back into me. Was I that pathetic or what? I looked at my book and realized that was what had tipped her off. I was reading a favorite, *Man's Search for Meaning* by psychiatrist Viktor Frankl.

This young lady literally judged a book — and me! — by its cover. Hardly a romantic thriller, it is, oddly, anything but depressing. I chuckled, a bit embarrassed by my sophomoric antics, and returned to Frankl.

Pages told of his ten months in the Auschwitz death camp during WWII. Words paled to describe one of the most horrific places ever conceived, a literal hell on earth. How could any book that came out of that experience be anything but bitter?

Frankl wrote one of the most inspiring works of this century. It is a profoundly insightful psychological study of man's ability to rise above circumstances no matter how horrid.

In the midst of insane Nazi brutality, Frankl found six men who stood above the rest. They seemed to possess an inner peace and sense of strength, dignity and purpose, traits lost by most prisoners once they passed through hell's gates.

He observed them conducting themselves in ways far different from others. Each morning, they set aside a portion of the watery potato "soup" and bread crust that would be their only rations for the day. Each evening, when they returned from forced labor, they sought out the weakest in the barracks, those too worn to work and even too sick to stand. With them they shared their hoarded food.

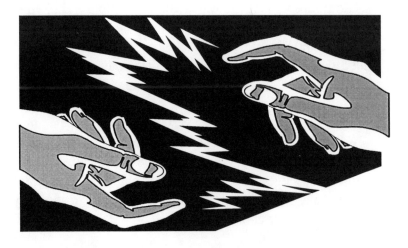

In a place where ability to do meaningful work meant a reprieve from the gas chamber, this extra nourishment meant life. Often Frankl observed his study group taking less fortunate souls with them to their bunks to give warmth and comfort during, what turned out for some, their last nights on earth. Death came with peace surrounded by loving, human warmth, a haven of comfort in the pits of hell.

There was no rational explanation for what Frankl observed. Why should men starve themselves by giving food to others who were going to die soon anyway? Nobody would have faulted them for not sharing. Indeed, no one would have even blamed them for *taking* food from those too weak to eat it themselves. After all, there was nothing they could do to forestall the fate that awaited their fellow prisoners who were already kissed for death. Why didn't they look out for Number One and survive the best possible ways they could?

Because, logic too was damned in that damnable place. As Frankl saw, the six not only survived, but persevered better than most. These six ordinary individuals were among the few still on their feet to greet their liberators.

Who could figure? After the war, Frankl took up the challenge to find the answer. He went over everything he had experienced and witnessed and then wrote *Man's Search for Meaning*. Frankl concluded that survival came because these men were able to sustain meaning in their lives through the exercise of *choice*.

Nazis might strip them of almost everything: their homes, families, jobs, wealth, status, and even their lives. But, as long as they still exercised choice in the precious few areas left to them, the enemy could never defeat them. They shared food because they chose. They comforted the dying because they chose. They survived because they chose.

By choice, they were able to sustain a dignity that far outbalanced the sustenance or warmth they gave away. In a most fantastic way, they ingested a different kind of nourishment. As perverse a pleasure as it appears, they were able to deny their captors the satisfaction of seeing them surrender.

———•———

Rising to a higher sense of humanity can bring triumph to everyday situations in our own lives.

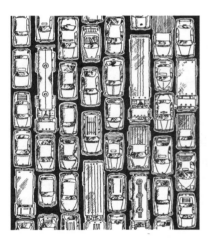

My wife, Joyce, has a knack for that. One time, when driving on the local bypass, she accidently cut off another motorist. Fuming, this guy raced to come alongside her. As luck would have it, side by side, they both stopped at the same red light. In a fit of apoplexy, he cursed, shook his fist, and made the usual anatomical gestures.

My wife nonchalantly rolled down her window. Instead of engaging this man in a contest of verbal abuse, she sweetly asked him how his wife and kids were doing. She said she was so sorry they had not gotten together for a while. "Be sure to say hello," she concluded.

Of course, she did not know him from Adam, but he didn't know that! Verbal carnage ceased. As far as he knew, Joyce would be on the phone with his wife in a few minutes, telling her what a dumb ass she was married to. He mumbled a weak apology; and as the light turned green, politely and red of face waited until Joyce drove away.

My darling spouse's sole source of inspiration was simple: she did not want to grant him satisfaction for ignoble deeds. Instead of letting him ruin her day, sending her home fuming and upset, she turned the tables. She did not *react*; she chose instead to just *act*.

Suppressing normal reaction is not an easy thing to do. I would have been stewing with resentment over the way he had overreacted. We both would have been cursing and shaking our fists at each other. Why does it seem we often make poor choices?

Years ago Scott Smith wrote an essay entitled *'Noble' Burdens Result in Forged Feelings.* He says that he grew up with a sense that he was supposed to carry great burdens throughout his life. Furrowed brows and long sighs indicated nobility and gave the impression one read the classics.

He labeled happy people as dumb or insensitive. When he was about 40, he decided his burdens of "nobility" were actually mockeries. He defeated this demon by effecting change through choice. He started slowly, one day at a time, until he found himself in a different and happier mode in his life.

Let me tell you about Bob, a fellow who, for most of his life, found himself in situations where he did not want to be. Though no scholar in high school, he went to college because he thought that was what was expected. Actually, he went to several colleges, graduating from none. He took a succession of white-collar jobs because he thought that was what was expected of him, too.

Success came in none.

By age 40, he was miserable with a resultant halo effect. Everyone around him — wife, children, mother, co-workers — was miserable, too. At the end of his rope and desperate, he shocked everybody by enrolling in a machine repair course. He came home each night with grease on his blue-collar shirt and dirt under his fingernails; but he was good at what he did and he was happy.

The people in his life quickly got over their shock at this sudden career change. Bob was surprisingly pleasant and, after securing a new job, made more money than ever. What caused this about-face?

"All my life, I tried to be something I wasn't," he said. "I strove to please everyone but myself. It didn't work. When I really looked deep inside, I realized the only time I had been happy was when I was working with my hands. I am what I am, and if people don't like it, too bad."

———— • ————

For two decades, I have been living and working in a unique corner of America, Pennsylvania Dutch country. German settlements go back to the early 18th Century, and there still exists a strong Germanic tradition and ethic.

The Pennsylvania Dutch are sturdy, hard-working, and inventive people. They pride themselves on their independence and ability to stoically accept life without complaints. But, there is a dark side, something that people around here have named the "Dutch Act."

The suicide rate among the Pennsylvania Germans is significantly higher than the national average. The culture makes it difficult for people to talk about what bothers them. When they can not take it anymore, they commit the Dutch Act and take themselves out.

That is a heavy price to pay for keeping things bottled up inside. But, it is entirely in keeping with what medical literature has to say about stress and suicide. In addition to making us miserable and depressed, we know that repression of feelings and exposure to inordinate amounts of anger and frustration weakens our immune system. This increases risks multi-fold for illnesses, from heart disease to cancer and multiple other maladies.

We also know that by paying attention to what our mind and body tell each other, positive, measurable medical benefits can be achieved. Let me give you an example.

On the physical side, we all know about runner's high. The brain releases morphine-like chemicals called endorphins during the stress of strenuous exercise. These neurotransmitters not only ease the pain of extreme exertion but turn it into a sensuous pleasure. Additionally, through the use of biofeedback, techniques can be taught to call upon those same endorphins to ease chronic pain.

Psychologically, we know there is no peace of mind, no ease from grief, and no self esteem without self awareness. We talk so much about getting in touch with our feelings that it becomes trite. Unfortunately, what we know to be best for us is not always what we do. Perhaps times are changing, but most of us are still in old traps.

Big boys don't cry. Girls aren't supposed to get angry. None of us is supposed to lose control. Many feelings are still considered off limits — sins in thought and word carry as equal weight as the despicable deed itself. We go through life burdened with guilt, which puts us under an enormous handicap.

Like Bob, we spend years not knowing who we are or what we want. We succumb because we are unable or unwilling to acknowledge what we truly feel about ourselves. Currents of *shoulds* and *oughts* carry us down narrower and narrower channels of happiness and opportunities.

———— • ————

Cancer is an integral part of my practice. Regardless of the severity of people's diseases, how well they do depends upon how well they cope. Many have never permitted themselves to become close to their feelings. Now, they are suddenly forced to deal with an onslaught of unexpected emotions.

Friends, some family members, and acquaintances tell me the word "cancer" was not permitted to be spoken in their homes! Lisa, a young lady in our support group, was living at home while in college. She contracted a lymphoma and was trying her best to cope with the pressures of school and chemotherapy. "Dad and Mom absolutely refused to talk about my problems. We ate dinner, made small talk and walked around the house with a huge, fearsome gremlin at our side. We knew he was there but figured he would go away if we ignored him."

When Lisa had a recurrence in her chest months later, my friend, Grant Gordon, led her to our group, a safe haven for speaking of feelings, needs and unresolved conflicts.

Fear plays sentry in many people's lives. Unfortunately, we can be frightened to death. With fear in the vanguard, anger, depression, embarrassment and bitterness can join in ranks. These emotions can come in overwhelming undertows, pulling people in different directions and tearing them apart.

Part of our on-going group therapy includes keeping a daily journal. We encourage members to speak of feelings more than events. *How* events shape feelings becomes an essential part of understanding and furthering the progress of the patient.

Group members need to keep their bodies as strong and healthy as possible. They need to tap into their inner selves. They need to seek out paths that will guide them to their greatest fulfillment.

What did you feel when you had to tell your loved ones? Jot it down. *What does it feel like to lose your hair?* Make a note. *What fears, anxieties or regrets keep you from sleeping in the dark of night?* Write it down.

What is it that is keeping you from showing yourself in public?
What do you feel when you think about dying?

All feelings get recorded. When members are ready, they discuss journal entries at the support group. If anyone will understand, fellow members will. No one is alone. We are all on the same cruise ship. Some day, we will all die.

Sound easy? Verbal sharing is a method of doing what does not always come naturally to us, but it can be powerfully effective. What evolves from these journal discussions is not just acknowledgment of feelings but the realization that feelings are neither good nor bad. No matter what is said, response and feedback is non-judgmental. Guilt is not a member of our group.

SUPPORT GROUP MEMBER
Ever since I became ill, my spouse treats me like a China doll that might break with the slightest touch. I feel like screaming! I feel angry with her. I feel she doesn't understand. Then I feel guilty for feeling this way! So I just ignore my feelings.

SUPPORT GROUP
You are not a bad person for your thoughts. It's good to talk it out. If you just sit on it, that would be bad for you and your loved one. What you feel is not going to go away simply by trying to ignore it. It's what we call "the ostrich syndrome." If you can't see it, it can't hurt you. But it can.

Ignoring feelings leads to explosions that may have nothing to do with the resentment and ill feeling that caused the problem in the first place. Instead of telling your wife what you really want — that you're not so fragile and you need to be held and hugged now more than ever — you are likely to fight often over things trivial like what's for supper.

We cannot expect others to read our minds, especially if we, ourselves, have trouble reading what is in it. The group and journal are critical to helping members look inside themselves to gain insight, understanding and peace.

With issues in the open, they can be addressed. Freed of resentment and anger, members are empowered to makes choices to get what they need and to make the best of their situation.

The Multiple Sclerosis Society asked me to give a workshop on attitude. I slipped into the rear of the auditorium with hundreds of MS victims to hear the first speaker, a nationally known radio announcer and well-considered family therapist. Unknown to most, including myself, was that he was a quadriplegic. I was stunned. Here sat this young man in a quad chair, speaking to a group with whom he could certainly identify.

Covering his hand was a Velcroed glove and to the glove was stuck a similarly Velcroed coffee cup. At times during the talk, Dan would sip coffee, an obvious effort for a high thoracic quadriplegic.

"Don't you just hate it," he said, "when people see you in a wheelchair or on crutches and they want to treat you differently? I do. The other day I'm in the lobby of a hospital waiting to take the elevator to my office. I'm enjoying my coffee, just like I am now," he motioned to his cup with his head. "Some lady comes up and with a woeful waggle of her head, sorrowfully reaches into her pocket and puts a dollar in my cup!" The place roared.

"That's my damn coffee!" I shouted. "Well, the lady freaked. She could not clean my cup and get me a fresh one fast enough. But I must tell you," he concluded, "it really irked me when she said she wanted her dollar back!"

I found myself along with most of the others in the room in a fit of laughter. Here was a man who clearly had made choices: Laugh at life's jokes, even from a quad chair; bring sunshine and hope to yourself and hundreds of other joy-starved people.

──────◆──────

Donna is one of the most active, enthusiastic members of S.E.E.K. Though she does not have cancer, she more than qualifies for inclusion. She suffers from a bladder and kidney ailment that has changed her life. With more than a hundred hospital admissions in the last ten years, last year she spent more days in the hospital for a variety of infections than she did at home. I have personally operated on her more than 25 times — and I am not her primary physician.

So much of her has been surgically altered or rearranged that she can no longer eat or drink by mouth. She constantly fights infection and pain. She has lost inner ear function, the key to body balance. As a result, simple acts like walking or sitting up are great chores.

How has all this affected her? As little as she can possibly make it. She is an active wife, mother and homemaker. She is in constant contact with other S.E.E.K. members and, like a big sister, lends a helping hand, a reassuring word, or a shoulder upon which to cry. All this for others who struggle through their own crises as she fights through hers.

She is able to triumph because she came to terms with her infirmities and is determined to work around them to live life the best she can. Even the days when she cannot stand up without falling over, she never lets setbacks get her psyche down. She adapts. She does not have to be able to stand to have a productive day. She can always work the phone or take care of correspondence in a horizontal position.

Donna rarely does or thinks in halfway terms. As far as she is concerned, calamity has not made her less of a person, nor reduced her capabilities in any significant way.

"There is no living and there is no dying," she insists. "You are either alive, or you're dead." And as long as she is not dead, she has every intention of being just as alive as anyone can be.

Talk about an incurable romantic!

Wellsprings

Whether you think you can, or
you think you can't, you're right.

Vive la Difference

Don't bemoan the fact that you have fat thighs.
Celebrate your fat thighs! Find a fat thigh lover!
F. Leo Buscaglia, University of Southern California teacher,
and facilitator of "Love" class 101

It is in affliction that we are made to endure.
Endurance leads to lasting virtue and virtue to hope.
Paul's letter to the Romans

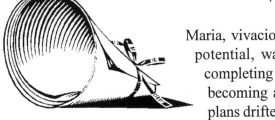

Maria, vivacious, pretty and full of potential, was a medical student completing her lifelong dream of becoming a doctor. Graduation plans drifted happily through her mind as she exited a book store and stepped off a curb into the path of a careening sedan. The drunk driver's car slammed Maria's body into the pavement. During that instant of horror, she knew her fate would be worse than death.

Months at the rehab center were a blur. Each day would start with an angry litany against a God who would allow her to become a quadriplegic. "All I ever wanted was to be a doctor, a healer! And *You* let this happen! How can I survive with people dragging my body from place to place?" she would anguish.

She alienated everyone — doctors, family, friends. Visitors were few. Her caregivers were filled with great trepidation.

One day a young man, also a quad, was wheeled in by a nurse. He had been injured in a diving accident at a shallow town fountain — teenagers having a good time. Alcohol and poor judgment once again had brought tragedy.

Maria glared at this intrusion and rudely looked away when he spoke. "Maria, if God wanted you to be another Michael Jordan, He would have made you six foot nine. Instead, He *let* you become a quadriplegic. So why don't you go out and be the best quad you can be. Or hurry up and die. Because you're wasting a lot of your own and other people's time."

Maria slowly turned her head to look at this brash young man, but he was already on his way out the door. He got her thinking and not just blaming. Slowly, she found things she could do. She taught herself to paint again with her mouth holding the brush. And the pictures this girl could paint! Her canvases spoke of freedom to run again through nature. They showed parties and dances and quiet moments with friends.

Then Maria taught others with severe neurological deficits. Now she says, "*Even though* people have to move my body from place to place, I still have purpose, goals and meaning." She may very well be doing more healing for herself and others than she would have as a doctor.

Maria is a healer because she discovered the gift of uniqueness. Her entire life had been a path towards a goal that suddenly terminated at a steep cliff. Her only choice was a long, treacherous path. She chose to go forward and seek unique possibilities instead of giving up and becoming embittered over what might have been.

Life is difficult for all — rich, poor; brilliant, average; healthy, physically challenged — but common threads run through us all.

Conformity and "fitting in" is painfully important throughout our lives. Remember those teenage years when we were a cloned mass of music, hair, lingo and clothes? To be different was the kiss of doom. As we grew older, we hopefully became more self assured and realized that we needed to celebrate our own uniqueness so that self discovery could occur. How can being different or unique help us survive and grow?

Genetics dictates some fascinating, scientific rules. The human race is the biggest outbred population of creatures on the face of the planet. Of the countless possibilities dictated by our nucleic acids, chromosomes and genes, it is virtually impossible to find two people the same. The lone exception, of course, are those who have shared the same womb. Even then, environment brings uniqueness.

The Creator responsible for this ingenious method of creation has tied into this chemical combination a blueprint for productivity and potential. Who you are is no accident. We all have a different role to fulfill for humankind to reach its completion. Imagine! In order for the story of mankind to be complete, you and I must discover and fulfill our own uniqueness. Discovering our own singular purpose makes it possible for growth, maturity and meaning to take place.

The meaning of life is to make a positive difference for having been alive. "I was here! I mattered!"

The source of courage to fulfill life's mission comes from within. Answers to all the tough questions lie inside. All we need do is listen to this inner, life-giving spirit. The key to peace, happiness, contentment? . . . Look inside.

Hear the words of teacher and author, Susan Jones. "It seems today that many people are searching for the fountain of youth. For that magic secret which will enable them to live a rich and full life. With happiness and longevity as the goal, emphasis has been placed upon special diets, supplements and exotic foods or exercise. Yet few people seem to look deeply enough to understand that the secret of living a quality life, full of aliveness, full of joy and satisfaction, comes from within. Through our attitude, through our expression, through our thoughts, and how we view ourselves and the world around us."

We are responsible if our lives appear drab and senseless, full of the tedium that comes with daily routine. If the joy is gone, then change the music. "Life is a daring adventure or it is nothing!" said inspiring, unique Helen Keller. We have our brush, we have our colors, we paint paradise, and then we go in.

Specialness, yours and mine, helps us survive in a world of seeming injustice. Uniqueness permits us to start the day looking in the mirror and seeing singular beauty. Believe it! It is the only way to live. The alternative is despair, decay, and death of spirit.

Love and hope lead us back to ourselves. Through self discovery, we find the best "me." Celebrating and nurturing our uniqueness support our daily, mundane struggles. When tragedy occurs, our sense of worth buoys us like a life preserver in a stormy sea. Specialness rescues us from monotonous, meaningless existence.

Anonymous, from a graduation program book.

I'm Special

I'm special. In all the world there's nobody like me.
Nobody has my smile.
Nobody has my eyes, nose, hair or voice.

I'm special. No one laughs like me or cries like me.
No one sees things as I do.
No one reacts just as I would react.

I'm special. I'm the only one in all of creation who has my set of abilities. My unique combination of gifts, talents and abilities are an original symphony.

I'm special. I'm rare.
And in all rarity there is great value.
I need not imitate others.
I will accept — yes, celebrate — my differences.

I'm special. And I'm beginning to see that God made me special for a very special purpose. God has a job for me that no one else can do as well as I do. Out of all the applicants only one is qualified. That one is me.
      Because . . . I'm special.

Reader's Digest tells the story of a boy born blind and retarded who was abandoned at a Milwaukee hospital. Officials sought foster parents for Baby John Doe. Finally they found May Lempke and her husband. "Care for him a little while. He'll probably die young anyway," they were told. May responded, "If I take him he won't die young, and I'm happy to care for him." Renamed "Leslie," the baby grew and so did the Lempkes' problems. His responses were flat and the foster parents carried him from place to place. Years passed. One day, May observed Leslie plucking a string on a package. She thought he might be responding to the vibrations and perhaps music would stimulate him even more.

She surrounded Leslie, now a teenager, with music of every kind from classical to rock. They even put an old piano in his room and May would move Leslie's fingers along the keys. Still there was no response. All this brought frustration and tears. The elderly Lempkes wondered if they had made the right decision.

Then, one night they were awakened by someone playing a Tchaikovsky's piano concerto. They ran to Leslie's room and to their amazement, found him sitting at the piano and playing beautifully! Music came from a child who had never played one key on his own let alone gotten out of bed before!

You see, Leslie was an autistic savant. Information had been absorbed and digested, but because of his condition, he could never express back, that is, until now. Parental love allowed that final expression of uniqueness.

Often, patients with terminal illness show up at our support group looking for a magic elixir. They expect something uncommon to prevail, and it does, except not always in the manner anticipated. That reality may be why many new clients leave disappointed. They do not allow enough time to discover that the key to obtaining "magic" lies in discovering their own self. Most of us are short on the required patience it takes to make that inner trip. But my friends in the support group have learned to cope and to deal courageously with their difficulties. They continually strive to become all they can be. They know time is too short.

We all play games sometimes. We pretend life would be perfect if we were someone else, Cindy Crawford maybe or Joe Montana. But only *They* can be the best *Them!* You need to find the best *You* in order to find your place in the universe. Only then will you unearth the touchstone of true joy and contentment. Inner peace happens sometimes in ways we can never predict. Sometimes we find ourselves by losing ourselves . . . through afflictions like quadriplegia or cancer.

Father Tony DeMello, a Jesuit educator, prays, "For all that has been. Thanks. To all that shall be. Yes!"

The first ten years of Fran's life were straight Main Street U.S.A. — a bike, a dog, ice cream, and faded blue jeans. Then juvenile diabetes was diagnosed. At first, his life was minimally interrupted with insulin shots and doctor checkups. Fran still brimmed with enthusiasm and gusto. What made him madder than hell, though, was when people treated him differently. When he reached his twenties, his condition began having serious effects on his chosen career of medicine. School after school rejected him not because he was not qualified, but because they all predicted his severe diabetes would leave him blind.

Finally, Temple University in Philadelphia gave him a seat in their school of medicine. He graduated near the top of his class. It looked as if the prophecy of sightlessness would be wrong, but in the middle of his residency, Fran abruptly lost his vision. Finishing his residency, he took time to learn Braille and train a seeing eye dog. Fran became the first blind doctor to ever pass the difficult Internal Medicine Board Exam.

His patients love him. He "sees" in ways that others of us in the profession could never have sensed. His love of people and his uniqueness brought to him great accomplishment and to his patients vast healing. Fran has undergone cardiac surgery for blood vessel disease hastened by his diabetes. Yet, he continues to triumph in healing himself and others. He now heads a hospital geriatric department. The elderly, especially those demented with such diseases as Alzheimer's, respond to his loving touch, and his zest for life.

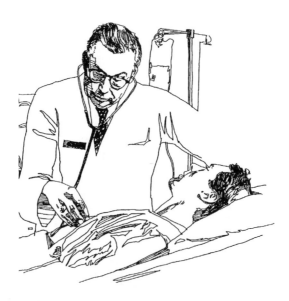

———•———

Maria, Leslie, Fran, all of us are the distillates of centuries of evolution. We are the best we can offer the world. Too many of us deny our differences as sources of growth because we may perceive ourselves as just that . . . different.

We need to celebrate our unique differences and understand our value. If we do, we will be better prepared to complete our journey.

Touchstones

Drop in unexpectedly on an old friend.
Pay the toll on the turnpike for the car behind you.
Keep a journal.
Volunteer.
Take a walk through nature.
Buy lemonade from a child at a roadside stand.
Compliment someone on a home cooked meal.
Hold the door open for the person behind you.
Let somebody in front of you in traffic.
Smile at a total stranger.
Thank a teacher.
Keep in touch with your relatives.
Spend time with an elderly person.
Play Candyland with a child.
Give a loved one a hug.
Sleep in on a Saturday morning (or take a nap).
Watch Saturday morning cartoons.
Plant a flower.
Buy a box of crayons and use them often.

... Seeds of the Best

If you find yourself unable to change, you've lost the ability to grow. Without growth, you will never need to fear death because you're dead already!

Albert Einstein

Two angels visited me today.

Not the kind with wings or flowing white robes of Renaissance paintings. Though I am sure these two lovely young ladies would have looked sprightly in such a garb. These angels came upon me as I was doing yardwork at the edge of my property, which abuts land used by walkers, cyclists and joggers. It is a joyful, soothing sanctuary bordered by a babbling stream and ancient red oaks, the perfect place to escape the hectic pace that surrounds this greenbelt.

As our paths crossed, I was struck by the enthusiasm and excitement that greeted me from these two charming strangers. They somehow knew who I was. We made small talk about the gorgeous day, the lush foliage, and the nice planting job I was doing along my fenceline. I sensed that there was another reason for their presence.

Soon these messengers spoke of a dear, old friend, a surgeon, whom I had not seen for over twenty five years. Having a terrible personal problem, his faith was sorely being tested.

"He needs a renewal of your friendship,"
they said. That was all.

They delivered their missive, waved good-bye and were gone. Who they were or where they came from, I have no idea. I have not seen them since.

I called my friend, who was indeed in trouble. We spent a long time discussing our past and his present. Symbiosis. We were renewing forces for each other that day. I'm not sure that his problem will ever be completely resolved, but it was wonderful to speak to him again and I think he felt the same way.

Life is a Journey. Peck, Siegel and others have reminded us of this in many different ways. Our path to completeness crosses many others' paths, which carry individuals ripe with potential for bringing light and meaning. Conversely, we have the power to touch and to reach out to others even though we will never fully understand the parts we play. It is a ripple effect, the shores touched by our presence in the water both unseen and unnamed.

The future is always in kinetic motion, hard to discern yet waiting to become what we make of it. That's why the present should be treasured and tended more carefully. It is *now* and can be sculpted. The present is a certainty. It exists like a shiny coin in a pocket waiting to be spent. Yes, time is constantly in flux. Change is the only certainty.

Have you ever seen the card sharp poster of W. C. Fields? Suspiciously peering over the top of his hand, he holds his cards close to his chest, daring anyone to cheat by stealing a glance.

Too many people live their lives like that poster. Close to the vest. Hedging bets. Not risking, not living, not accepting any possibility of change. Not doing anything really productive. Waiting. For what?

We have been taught that unless we change, we will be left behind to revisit yesterday's menu again and again and again. People who have their heads on straight about life in general, know how to go with the flow and adapt to change. Indeed, some even master and control it. Those who are terminally ill come to recognize that change can be valuable if they use it to learn and grow.

When bad things happen, as they do to everyone, we have choices. *Rant and rage!* or *Roll over and play dead!* or *Embrace and explore!* The truly enlightened look at changing situations and ask, "What can this possibly teach me? How can I use this for growth and opportunity?"

I once heard a Las Vegas comedian named Joe Kogel speak. He had the misfortune of contracting malignant melanoma and several inches of his skin were removed and replaced by grafts. Realizing that a new ministry awaited him, he worked the "Kogel Effect" into his routine. Its message was that the worst things that happen in your life can become *seeds of the best*. His descriptions of dealing with doctors, hospitals, insurance companies, and other patients in his dilemma were touching and riotous. He got people's attention with his gift for humor and then gently delivered his message with great success.

Life holds many surprise gifts. If we do not open ourselves up to accept these gifts, then life becomes boring and meaningless. "Life's a banquet," Auntie Mame reminds. "But, most damn people are starving to death!" Open the package, tear off the ribbon, and see what surprises await you. Even bad things can be worthwhile.

If we really think about it, 99% of our lives are just fine. Most of us eat more than we need, are well-clothed and comfortably sheltered, and live long, productive lives relatively safe and free. Yet we become complacent and in a quagmire at times. We usually detest changes in our lives even before we explore whether or not they can help us grow.

Few of us, though, take the risk and accept the challenge of growth within our current circumstances. We stagnate. "I'd rather feel pain than nothing at all," said playwright Thornton Wilder.

Erich Fromm says, "Most of us die, before we are ever fully born." The paths upon which we find ourselves, either by choice or by mandate, are where we must bloom. We must realize that even the rugged path can have great value. For example, death can be a marvelous teacher. It shows us that life must be treasured and lived urgently. It also teaches us not to hold on to anything too tightly. Crisis can be a danger signal and an opportunity.

Talk to someone living with metastatic cancer. Find out how his or her life is being lived. If you suddenly contracted a fatal disease, would you change the way you are living? Sadly, for many of us the answer is "Yes!"

Why does the imminent threat of death have to be the greatest prodder? We need to embrace change <u>now</u> as part of living and accept change as a cornerstone of growth. Does death have to be the one to nudge us out of our nests of complacency? We need to *straighten up and fly right* while we are still healthy and robust.

My patient and friend Patty knew about change, but she also knew she had lots of control over her life. After mothering a houseful (35!) of adopted and foster children, she developed breast cancer. Throughout her illness, she functioned normally as the kind, loving mother she was. Her last child was uniquely special. Mentally disabled and dependent, Patrick needed a great deal of extra help and love. He was still at home when Patty's condition worsened.

Her strength and perseverance came through. For years — not the months doctors thought — she continued to survive, and remarkably so. Her metastatic disease waxed and waned but never seemed to get the best of her body. Until Patrick was settled with an older sibling, she confided, she would not give in.

Finally, he was able to go live with his sister. A call came from the family that Patty was back in the hospital and her prognosis looked bleak. I arrived on the oncology floor to witness a brave friend, barely alive, hardly breathing. The nurses asked if I could do the family a favor. Of course! Anything!

This event was during the Persian Gulf War and Patty's oldest son was heading to Saudi Arabia. Could I arrange to have him see his mother one last time? I called the Red Cross right away.

For two days, I was unable to get to Patty's room. Her son had come, spent time with his mother and left for overseas. I went to say belated good-byes to Patty, fearfully expecting that I may have been too late.

I was not prepared for what I saw. I went in and, seeing a tall lady sitting by the bed voraciously downing a huge breakfast, I feared the worst had happened and the room was already filled with a new occupant. "Dr. Frangipane!" a strong voice called my name. It was Patty looking as well as I had ever seen her! She had made an unpredicted turnabout overnight. She joyfully told me of her son's visit. He would be okay, she felt, and Patrick, too, was thriving. The family was settled.

I stood and told her I would be back. Her smile to me held such peace. She picked up my hand, as though I were the one who needed comfort. "No, my friend," she said gently. "Now is my time to leave." She died a few days later, full of peace and fulfillment.

I love the wisdom of John Taylor, a Unitarian minister, who said:

There is stark beauty in the life well-lived, filled with adventures and misadventures. We may well curse our problems and wonder what evil scheme sends us on journeys to great heights and precipitous depths, but we should also consider the variety and beauty of it all.

Problems are not only stumbling blocks in our lives; they also are milestones marking our continuing development. These events . . . stimulate our mind and life to achieve new, undreamed of heights. Few of us want problems, but how limited we would be without them. Even fewer of us would eagerly taste the bitter fruit of defeat, but without the losses how could we recognize the joy of victory? We would surely seek escape from tragedy for its pain is too much for us, yet we can emerge from the most heartbreaking experience with a new grasp and wonder and love of life.

Every problem had hidden within it a rewarding potential. To recognize and use this truth is to make existence worthwhile and give every tomorrow the rich gift of today.

A life filled with change that sometimes leads to catastrophe and tragedy can be an opportunity for blessing. Meeting adversity is a refining process that makes us a mature, complete person. Looking back on our lives, it is the "bad" things that really were our best teachers. Hitting the lottery would give few of us new insight. And I am certain it would not teach me anything new, since most of us are already pretty good at spending money! But, ah, the bad things have volumes to teach.

Life is a process. We are introduced to all the wonder and beauty in the form of *possibilities*. If we examine the mystery, we can unlock doors and go inside to truly experience. One of life's puzzles is how adversity, despair, travesty and injustice — ugly, deformed looking *seeds* we want to immediately reject — can lead to development and flowering. Struggle can give birth to freedom, growth and meaning.

In high school, I painfully tried to master geometry and calculus. I was determined to understand and was proud of my achievement when it finally came. But, it came with great anguish and mental stretching. Eventual understanding and success went a long way in alleviating the discomfort.

Once an accomplishment is achieved, our appetite is whetted. We get that personal high, which bolsters us for new challenges. Wimp begets wimp. Mastery begets mastery. The choice is ours. But this involves the final and most important step in the process. Commitment.

Bill Bradley, in speaking of his Princeton basketball days, remarked that once he found himself on top, the next step was trying to figure out how to stay there. Commitment brings staying power. It helps us dig trenches, bulwarks and stockades to protect turf hard fought and won. It reinforces the gridwork and underpinnings of life. Pity the fainthearted who back away from challenge and adversity. Their crystalline foundation has little resilience and ability to withstand inevitable blows and hard knocks.

Change. Evolution. Growth.
All necessary for completeness.
All vital for healing
and life
and growth.

Wellsprings

No farmer ever plowed a field
by turning it over in his mind.

Lighten Up

Most people are about as happy
as they make up their minds to be.
Abraham Lincoln

God laughs, it seems, because He knows
how it all turns out in the end.
Harvey Cox

Ellen and Allen came to see me when she discovered a lump in her breast. This wonderful couple supported each other through a tough year of cancer, surgery, radiation and harsh chemotherapy.

Their strongest weapon, invincible shield, stalwart defense line? Humor . . . and of course a vast, backup phalanx of wit, irony, laughter, spoofing, jokes, pranks, guffaws and chortles!

At first, my concern was that they were in a state of denial and camouflaging fear and anger with false bravado. Their strong, visible sense of joy with the world must be a smoke screen. No one could possibly be that happy all the time.

As I've gotten to know Ellen and Allen, I realize that this joyfulness is how they truly are. Through life's peaks and valleys, they actively seek humor to buoy their spirits and give to those about them a wonderful sense of the hilarity of life.

After she received *The Call* (Ellen's tagline) from me with news of her cancer, Ellen decided that humor would exist even after breast cancer. They both insisted one can never fully know humor without first experiencing sorrow or tragedy.

This delightful couple landed in eastern Pennsylvania from the Bronx. Our strong ethnic backgrounds bonded us instantly. "How do you say 'Hello' in the Bronx?" Ellen asked upon our first meeting. "I don't know," I replied. "Stick 'em up!" she said in her best James Cagney. I thought I grew up in a tough neighborhood!

Office visits with this Burns and Allen duo were adventures. She dealt with her problems "outrageously." Blood drawing was done by *vampires*, and she always smiled broadly for the myriad of x-rays "pictures." Chemotherapy was her strategy for fitting into a Size 9 again. Alas, when prednisone, a weight-gaining steroid was prescribed, out the window flew svelte figure dreams.

Nearly bald from chemotherapy, Ellen sometimes wore a turban and called herself *The Swami*. I was treated to a different "fright" wig each office visit.

She managed dramatically and well. Her cheer was contagious. We felt it in our office for hours after she left, smiling at a joke she told as we were reminded of the punch line. Her fresh breeze attitude lingered long after she was gone.

Ellen and Allen are not naive, ignorant people who bury their heads in the sand. Quite the contrary! Highly motivated and perceptive, they know that for them to deal with this catastrophe and have any hope of survival, humor *must* be involved. There was no *on-the-other-hand*. They looked square into the face of cancer and did not see death, pain and sorrow. Instead, they caught a glimpse of growth potential. They seized the opportunity with laughter, joy and chuckles.

Comedian Dr. Joel Goodman states that *exceptional people —* survivors — use humor to prevent "hardening of the attitudes." Good cheer and mirth help re-frame the unattractive, cope with the unexpected, and smile through the unbearable. Allen and Ellen Charney are living proof.

———— ◆ ————

I used to get insulted when I first came to this part of eastern Pennsylvania to practice medicine. It is populated by a hearty stock of German people referred to as "Dutch." Their Germanic and my romance language stems mixed poorly. People fractured my last name, and so I learned to respond to anything that came even moderately close.

Dr. Frank-In-Pain was not a name to hang on a shingle.

Dr. French Panties was a moniker given by an elderly, diabetic lady whom I sang to during her amputation. She later gave me a ukulele engraved with that nickname so that I might perform the next surgery with an accompanist!

Dr. Fran Gee. Dr. Fractured. Dr. Fancy Pants (my favorite).

One elderly lady asked about my nationality. When I replied that I was Italian-American, she looked shocked. She thought I was Japanese. *Dr. Fran-Japan.*

Hey, I had a choice! Fume and steam because people messed up my name . . . or have some fun. If I dismissed my frustration with a grand Italian hand flourish and shoulder shrug, the awkward moment when someone butchered my appellation became our joke. Lessening their embarrassment and softening my annoyance, levity became an icebreaker and put us both at ease. It showed my humanity by being able to laugh at myself.

Comedian Jerry Seinfeld says, "The whole object of comedy is to be you. The closer you get to that, the funnier you will be." The funniest thing about human beings is precisely that we take ourselves too seriously.

Get up each morning and do — preferably naked — a little mirror therapy. Admire (!) your body and say, "You sweet old thing!" If your reaction is like mine, you will laugh hysterically. If you don't develop the ability to laugh at yourself, the rest of the day (rest of your life!) will be a bummer.

For me, that moment when I have to look at myself naked cannot get any worse. Or, if I can laugh, any better.

———•———

Frank was hospitalized for metastatic colon cancer. During rounds, I found him nauseated, without appetite and listless. "How are you Frankie?" I asked. "Well, Doc," he began. "This is the shits. It's a little like falling off a forty-story building. As

I pass the twentieth floor, some lady leans out the window and asks me 'How ya doin'?!' So I say, 'Oh, I'm okay — so far!'" Frank chose to see the humor in his predicament. Things could always be worse. He had not hit the sidewalk yet.

My father dealt with lymphoma and prostatic malignancy in the same year. They were, he said, "his" illnesses. He did not lay his problems like a huge "boulder of guilt" upon my mother or anyone else. Instead, he chose to enhance and fortify his already strong, joyful personality.

His daily trips to radiation oncology brightened everyone's day. Technicians, nurses and doctors recognized this remarkable man's drive and zest for life. His trips became adventures, and he refused to allow others to drag him down. He responded to depressing news with jokes or quips that brought hearty laughter. He lived Norman Cousins' philosophy: "Laughter is a form of internal jogging." Good for the heart and certainly good for the immune system.

Many of Cousins' books speak of the positive effects of laughter. *Anatomy of an Illness*, his most famous, relates how his very survival as a child in a tuberculosis ward hinged on sharing play and joy with fellow patients. Today, in part because of slowly changing attitudes brought about by pioneers like Cousins, hospitals are finally changing their rigid formality. Oncology floors resemble family "living" rooms where patients can watch videos of comedies, cartoons and TV sitcoms.

Laughter has an indisputable, positive effect on the body's Surveillance Department, the immune system. It can raise T-cell counts and stimulate red cell production in the bone marrow. The therapeutic touch concept in vogue today full of hugging and touching (which laughter does *internally*) are not new treatment modalities. Healers the world over have known the benefits of touch and humor for centuries. Mothers instinctively know. Yes, like touching, humor is strong medicine.

Do not tell me that an illness, even as bad as cancer, cannot be a laughing matter.

———————•———————

Philip Butler, a Vietnam POW, survived months of grueling captivity. Asked how he found the fortitude to survive such an ordeal, Phil replied, "Optimism and humor are the grease and glue of life. Without both of them we would never have survived our captivity."

I am convinced, as I observe the people in my practice, that using humor to build a positive attitude is essential to survival. As I travel the country speaking about my life as a physician, I meet many who bear witness to humor's importance.

Suzanne Honeycutt worked years in a Kentucky hospital, developing a program called "Oasis" where patients, their families and friends gathered to watch TV and movies, read, snack and just talk. Suzanne brought the relaxed, comfortable, healing atmosphere of a good home into the hospital. Using her work as an inspiration, she conducts humor workshops called exercises in "FUNdamentals."

Using everyday events as a source of humor, she encourages others to experience their own humanity as a wellspring of delight. She humorously exposes her own foibles and frail humanity. One of my favorite stories is her constant, uncanny ability to get lost. She calls herself "geographically dyslexic." I roar at the troubles and circumstances that occur surrounding her misadventures.

Patients, in the strangest garbs, come to my office. One, a professional clown, lost a leg to diabetic gangrene. Richard dealt with his problem by bringing mirth to others through buffooning. He appeared in my office in full clown array for my fortieth birthday. Somehow he coerced my father and a stripper to come along. To say the least, it was not a ho-hum day at the office! My father, by the way, enjoyed all this activity the most.

Do I have a wonderful bunch of patients or what!? . . .

Some show up wearing rubber noses.

Some write *interesting* notes on various parts of their anatomy. Imagine a scrubbed and garbed surgical team bending over the abdominal note of an anesthetized patient:

Make incision here!

Other patients' body notes tell what to TAKE OUT or how much to TAKE IN as if I were a tailor altering a fine suit.

I love it! This kind of humor is not perverse or out of place because it is done with gentleness and taste. These patients agree with the adage, *Humor may be hazardous to one's illness.*

Poets and philosophers say the greatest source of laughter is our own anguish. Mark Twain knew the "secret fountain of humor is not joy but sorrow." They speak the truth. The extra baggage and folly of self-importance never appears so frivolous as when facing one's own impending end.

———•———

Support group meetings bring forth more smiles than tears. Sounds of laughter cast greater ascending ripples than the sounds of weeping. Exceptional people are proof. One evening, two "terminally" ill people found themselves engaged in a pre-meeting conversation. As our meeting began, they stood at a far end of the room. One delightful member of our group glanced at them and remarked, "I guess they keep their distance because they think we have something contagious!"

Where does one find the strength of character to lighten up and make such humorous statements in the midst of travail? Perhaps enlightenment comes when we realize all of life contains potential sorrow and joy. Looking for happiness in the worst situations is not trite or trivialization. Indeed, it is medicine for the survival of one's spirit. Too many nonbelievers in the power of humor, however, continue to find flaws in even the best situations.

As Ellen says, "Life goes on with or without you. If you're going to take the ride, you may as well enjoy it."

Wonderful sentiment.
Perfect medicine.

Wellsprings

The longest journey is the journey inwards
of him who has chosen his destiny.
                    Dag Hammarskjold, *Markings*

Let's Get Metaphysical

Love whom I send you. I'll take care of you!
God, Creator of the Universe

It was a time of enormous professional growth and achievement. It was a time of enormous personal angst and questioning.

I was caught in the vortex of the proverbial best of times and worst of times. It is still difficult for me to mentally revisit and examine what happened.

I was part of a successful medical practice that was everything I had ever dreamed. Like the boy who grew up and finally got everything he wanted, I was going to live happily ever after. But there I was, outwardly successful in every sense that the world measures achievement, yet incredibly, I was terribly unhappy.

Within the framework of my daily practice, I felt little room to maneuver. I was locked in, bound by the rules of a jealously demanding, consummating profession. Medicine had become a mistress who was loathe to allow me to be free.

The basis of my unhappiness was never the outstanding professional team I was fortunate enough to work with. They supported and understood me as best they could. The real problem lay in my not realizing how my philosophical path was diverting from theirs.

Like a child leaving for college, I was in the midst of separation anxiety. I understood my journey needed to go in a different, more difficult direction. In a state of denial, I could not muster the courage to steer my ship out of the safe, secure channeling to which it had become accustomed. I refused to believe, much less accept the inner voice which told me change was necessary. I wanted to stay close, safe. But deep within me, the truth offered no relief. I knew that my course followed a separate way.

From where I stood, the path looked narrow, winding and steep. It was uninviting to say the least. I contemplated, sought counsel, prayed, and then announced my intentions to leave my secure professional world to chart paths unknown. To say I burned bridges was putting it mildly.

People who knew and loved me supported my decision to practice my career on my terms. Others saw it as a slap in the face. The uninformed believed the decision was made in haste, for insignificant, purposeless reasons. They laid a guilt trip on me for this seeming indignity towards those who had loved and nurtured me.

One of my best friends helped me understand that the correct decision had been made. "Leo," Vince said, "you're different!" We laughed at the obvious unintended double meaning. "No," he continued, "I really mean it. You have a separate peace to make. You've run your decision through your heart and head and it still comes out the same. Put it aside. Live it." He was right.

My resolution — to unchain myself from the restrictions of the way I approached my profession — was the correct one. It saddens me to know it hurt a lot of people. Never did I have that intention. What appeared on the surface to be a rejection of particular individuals was in reality an inward re-examination and redirection of myself. My life needed a new direction and this was the only way I could see myself through. It forever broke close ties, that to this day I still lament. I am still not sure that anyone completely understands my reasons, but in this book, I hope I can make known the continued deep love, respect and gratitude I hold for those who sustained me along the way. I've paid the toll for following my own road.

———•———

We come to the final chapter in this section and what I considered to be the most important. We have looked at many characteristics of survivors. They are responsible, exercise choice, and take calculated risks. They have a wonderful sense of humor, cheer their uniqueness, and know there is no relationship between productivity and aging. Of course, they recognize the need to live in the moment and concentrate on healing rather than curing. But the eminent attribute of these most remarkable individuals is their spirituality.

Spirituality.

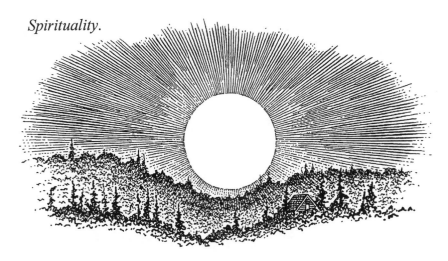

Do not confuse spirituality with religiosity, though they are inter-related. Spirituality is the ability to be introspective about our own nature, to seek a higher understanding.

Spiritual people do not suddenly awaken one morning to the fact that they are terminally ill and therefore need to start asking some serious, self-reflecting questions. These are individuals who have wondered about *who they are* and *where they came from* throughout their lives.

Spiritual dialogue asks:
> *What am I supposed to do with my life?*
> *Do I genuinely believe in a Supreme Being*
> *who is involved in the finite and material world?*
> *Where did I come from?*
> *What is death?*

Spiritual questions go far beyond rote answers in a catechism or Sunday school. Spirituality searches out meaning and purpose. *How much do I really believe in that philosophy or this explanation? Can I work it out myself? Do I need organized religion or philosophy to guide my hand?*

At the end of Cervantes' *Don Quixote*, we watch a dying hero explain the meaning of his life. In spite of all his seemingly insane activity, he still knew what he was supposed to do with his life. He pitied any man who reaches the moment of his death and asks, "Where lies life's path for me?"

There are many valid philosophies of life to which we can subscribe — Judeo-Christian, Buddhist, Hindu, Moslem to name a few. There is not just one exclusive religious path to choose for nurturing our spirituality.

Interestingly, many people profess to "believe" because they do not have the courage, again in Quixote's words, "to believe in nothing." Their belief is sort of *Spirituality by Omission*. When they contemplate their marvelous design and the universe about them, they profess to indeed believe in an Ultimate Creator.

But, *how* a Creator fashioned This Universe or That Being is far less important than *Now that I'm here, what am I supposed to do?* Actively using an inner Life Force to explore all these philosophical questions leads us to a much deeper *Spirituality by Commission*.

Years ago I came across a book, *Your God Is Too Small*, written by an Anglican minister. Most of us contemplate a Creator that is too impersonal, distantly removed, and far too vindictive. We put Him in a box and visit Him once a week for an hour or so, if He is lucky. We spend the rest of our lives living as if He only exists for those moments when we need Him.

Still others of us treat our God like an albatross about our necks, a constant reminder of some inborn unworthiness. We constantly make amends and beat our hearts in mea culpas. We may very well be unworthy, especially in comparison to the Creator, but a constant exhibition of guilt does little to bring about a spiritual resolution.

Siegel speaks of our God being either a hindrance or a resource. Box your God and pay only lip service to His bidding and you've become trapped and stung by a useless philosophy. But, utilize your God as a means for growth and question your own motives, nature and direction in the realm of your beliefs, and your God suddenly becomes a personal, essential part of living.

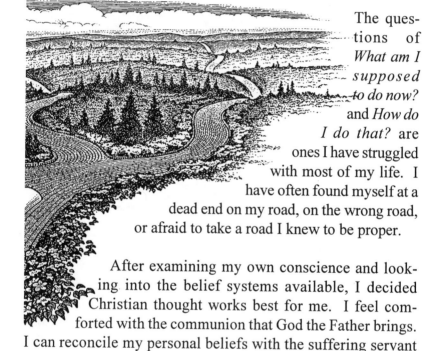

The questions of *What am I supposed to do now?* and *How do I do that?* are ones I have struggled with most of my life. I have often found myself at a dead end on my road, on the wrong road, or afraid to take a road I knew to be proper.

After examining my own conscience and looking into the belief systems available, I decided Christian thought works best for me. I feel comforted with the communion that God the Father brings. I can reconcile my personal beliefs with the suffering servant of God, Jesus, who redeemed me and all mankind with his saving act. However, there still are questions, searching and growth that need to occur before my faith and spirituality become as strong as I'd like.

I feel a great source of comfort with my beliefs.
It was not always so.

During the transition after I had left my secure medical practice and struck out on my own, my sense of security and direction was shaky and shattered. In a Vancouver church during a religious service, I found myself silently raging against my God.

Speaking to Him in my heart, I roiled over, "You've not made it very easy for me, you know! For *my* growth and *your* glory I made drastic changes in my life in order to practice my profession in a more loving, caring way. I felt like you sent me on a ministry — like I had a calling! But look what happened! My friends deserted me. One even thinks that I need a shrink — a psychiatrist! My life seems upside down! So here I am! Still unsure. Still uncertain! Am I heading the right way? What am I supposed to do?!"

What happened next was a transcendent experience which I shall never forget. I heard a "voice" and felt a presence unlike anything I had ever experienced before. In me. Through me. All about me. There was speech, but there was no voice. The message was kind, gentle, firm and resonate.

Love whom I send you.

That was the reply to my heart's anguished cry. Nothing more or less. The comforting power I felt erased hurt and anger, doubt and fear. Those five words certainly got my undivided attention, stopped my sniveling, and spiritually humbled me before The Great Healer.

Several months later in another church in California, I found myself asking a second question. "You know, I've been trying my best, but I still don't know for sure how I'm supposed to do this. Help me!" Same voice. Same Presence. This reply: "I'll take care of you." Five words again.

There's an index card with these two sentences, ten words, pinned to my bulletin board above my desk. When I need help or succor, I read it. I find comfort and reassurance.

———————•———————

Several years ago, my dear friend and patient, Mercedes Arnold, died of complications of breast and colon cancer. She was incredibly special, self-directed and honed in on her journey. This remarkable woman, guided by a strong core of spirituality, brought joy, encouragement and laughter to all she touched. When she could no longer travel to help others, she would lay in bed, use the telephone or write notes. She told me once that her God despised "inaction and ill humor in patients and doctors." Her life was a paradigm, a model for anyone wanting to live, love and achieve healing.

———————•———————

Texas internist Larry Dossey' book, *Healing Words,* speaks of the power of prayer in healing. His double-blinded study showed that those who are prayed for do much better than those who are not. The best  prayer he claims (and I agree) may be the most generic. It's the one that contains the phrase, "Thy will be done."

Recently, I encountered my profession from the other side of the bedrail when I underwent hip replacement surgery. I psyched myself up "that the operation and rehab would be a great adventure in putting all my proselytizing to the test. Could pain, inactivity and possible forced retirement give me growth and insight? Or were all my proclamations about healing, attitude and spiritualism just a sham from an old, snake oil salesman?

The week before my operation, an orderly whom I dearly love and appreciate came to me. Ernie is an unsung hero and sterling person who quietly creates excellence in his work sphere. His deep-felt religion and spirituality is no accident. "Frangi," he said. "Don't you worry about your surgery. I and 23 others are going to pray for you for the 24 hours on the day of your surgery. Each of us is taking an hour. You'll do just fine!"

I was overwhelmed. Through tears, I thanked him. I felt the power of an unconditional love that enabled Ernie and his friends to pray for me with great and natural ease. Imagine, most of these people did not even know me! I was just a fellow human being who needed intercession with the Creator. Theirs was an act of love. I felt safe — the dreaded scenarios in my mind marched off.

I was loved, cared for and healed by many people. I awoke from surgery without pain and have remained pain free through rehab. The love directed my way was laced with humor, encouragement, hope, reassurance and support. It was indeed a great adventure.

———◆———

Spiritual people, Dossey found, get well faster and deal with fear and anger more completely. They see their illness as a resource for growth.

Is spirituality an opiate merely used to control people? Don't believe it! It is rather a harbinger of inner piety and contemplation. Spirituality enables man to cradle hope while reaching for his glory.

Touchstones

Go in through the narrow gate, because the gate to
destruction is wide and the road that leads to it is easy,
and there are many who travel it. But the gate to life is
narrow and the way that leads to it is hard, and there are
few people who find it.

Matthew 7:13-14

Part 2

Outward
Bound

Getting Involved

Love is the ultimate expression of the will to live.
Thomas Wolfe, author

Have you ever peered inside a coffin?
Alongside the deceased, there are
sometimes trinkets or mementos left
by relatives or friends. A necklace.
A ring. Perhaps a poem or a favorite
item of the deceased. Sometimes it is
not what is placed in the coffin, but where the body is placed that
may be unique.

My dentist, Charlie Wolfe, was very close to his dad, an avid
fisherman. The elder Dr. Wolfe, also a dentist, wanted to be
cremated. When he died, his son decided to put the ashes in his
dad's favorite tackle box. He knew this would have delighted and
pleased the old man and it gave Charlie comfort in knowing this
was the perfect resting place.

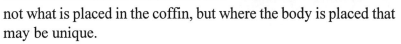

In spite of the vociferous objections of the local
undertaker, Charlie's desire was honored and
his dad rested with his favorite lures in "Old
Pal," his tackle box. Charlie meant no
disrespect. He strongly felt a need to express
his dad's genuine obsession and love of fishing.

After all, if people can be buried in their Cadillacs or Corvettes,
why not a tackle box? Ancient Egyptians surrounded their dead

with all kinds of paraphernalia for their trip to the next world.

Actually, there is only one thing we can take with us. Not fancy cars, or money, or favorite pets. Not our vacation home or social status or bank roll. Even Hollywood recognizes what this sole piece of carry-on baggage can be.

When I do public speaking, I ask audiences if they have ever seen one of my favorite movies, "Ghost." There is a character in that movie who looks *just like me!*, I tell them. Puzzled, they rack their brains. Some make guesses to be funny or polite. No, I say, it is not Demi Moore or Whoopi Goldberg. Then, I lay on them it's Patrick Swayze!

Stunned, embarrassed silence.

As they see that I am pulling their legs, a few chuckles turn into a room full of laughter. Okay, so this balding, over-the-hill Italian does not quite look like Mr. Swayze . . . (My wife would give you an argument.)

In that movie, our hero played by Mr. Swayze, has the last line. It sums up the main theme of the film. When the plot is resolved and the bad guys get their just desserts, there is a touching denouement. The hero, as he leaves along a stairway of light for the next world, turns to his lover. "Molly," he says. "All the love inside of me. It goes with me. I get to take it with me!"

Imagine. Our inheritance, the love compounded throughout life, goes with us! It is the only thing that matters and the only thing important enough to take along.

So essential, so important, so unique. Is it not crucial then to *get* and *give* as much precious love as possible? This section of the book deals with the importance of our love bank. The terminally ill have a passion for action and involvement. It is critical to their healing. The fervor of good will, which most of these folks exhibit, is a natural result of the self-directed mending discussed in the first part of this text.

Involvement is love turned outward. Loving others is an intuitive consequence of loving oneself.

———————•———————

Sam, a spiritual individual, often prayed and had a personal relationship with his Creator. He never asked for anything material, believing that God knew and would take care of all of his needs.

But, Sam and his family fell upon hard times. Financially he was in dire straits. One day he prayed, "God, if you could see it in your plans for me and if it wouldn't be too much trouble, could I win the lottery next Tuesday? Come on, give me a break!"

Well, Tuesday came and went with no big hit for Sam. Figuring he asked for too much, he modified his request. "God, me, Sam, again. How about giving me a break! Maybe the Cash 5 Mini Jackpot next Wednesday?" Well, nothing happened on Wednesday either.

Finally Sam prayed, "God, how about just a few hundred on the Daily Number next Friday? Give me a break!" With that, there was a flash of lightning and crash of thunder and God spoke. "Sam, give *me* a break! Buy a ticket!"

In our state, the lottery slogan is "You gotta play to win." Well, in life you never win unless you get involved. The power of interaction and involvement are what Sam didn't understand but what friends in the support group have taught me.

I am amazed at the networking that occurs without the slightest hint from any of the facilitators. Each and every one is there in a minute for any of the others. Personal difficulties are lovingly superseded while tending to the needs and troubles of others.

Liz is perfect example. Hampered by a severe neurologic disorder that leaves her nearly unable to walk, she nonetheless participates fully in life. Her sharp mind and caring nature allow her to touch people in other ways. She is our author and our note writer, always there with an encouraging word often written on a homemade card. I have personally received some of these along with a beautiful needlepoint sampler, which took her many times longer to make than the average person.

Profound. People faced with serious, life-threatening sickness recognize the need to get their own houses in order and then reach out to others with love and compassion. What characteristics of love enable this outreach? What characterizes *the involved*.

Unconditional Love

This trait allows me to identify in you that part that is like me. I recognize that you can become lonely, empty and unhappy just as I can and do. But there is also a part of each of us in which we share the essence of our humanity. This we seek when we love unconditionally.

This kind of love does not act expecting something in return. *I love you without strings. I do not want you to love me because I do something for you.*

Unconditional love risks the greatest chance of rejection. It opens us up to vulnerability. But it is, at the same time, the most difficult and wondrous of all forms of love. Eastern philosophy states that when we love each other unconditionally, we are each centered in that place where we are no longer two individuals, but one person. This is the purity of the act.

Transcendent Love

No bounds. Without limitation or shortfall. This involvement with others is all inclusive. Love of all people for their humanity. Doing for others because they are my brother or sister. "I love because they are my species," actress Ruth Gordon said.

This kind of love does not stop with people. It includes love and respect for all creation, be it animal or environment. Transcendent love understands that actions now show love and concern for those that come after. Life's bounty is but a loan for our temporary use. Payment comes through our careful use of what is given, our service to others.

Anonymous Love

Doing for others without drawing attention to self. "Let not the right hand know what the left is doing," the New Testament speaks to this issue. Truly committed, involved people need no congratulations or edification. Generous acts themselves are sufficient reward and fulfill the action of the doer.

My wife and I were involved in a group that took turns "courting" as a means of support. The group's couples all went through various tough times. Marriages may have been financially stressed. Perhaps a problem might involve a child. Whatever the situation, couples would find anonymous notes of encouragement tucked in their mailbox or by their front door. They were left by others of us who had experienced similar difficulties.

These notes were quite simple, yet the magic they held was the reassurance that said, "We've been there, too. We've hurt too. You have our love, support and prayers."

Simple acts were all that were needed. It did not matter from whom the notes came only that others cared and were supportive.

Spontaneous Love

Tied in with all the qualities above, surprise love includes the unexpected. Call that child at college in the middle of the night. "Honey, I love and miss you!" They will think you have flipped! Send flowers to your husband for no good reason. Leave love notes in a lunchbox. All of these things are unexpected gifts of joy. My how they get us through the day!

Author Napoleon Hill says, "Happiness is found in doing, not merely possessing." There are lots of anecdotes about how doing for others can literally change the way we physically feel ourselves. A group of patients with serious musculoskeletal disorders participated in an interesting study. Each member was tested objectively by ergometers for strength in various muscle groups. Half were asked to continue their usual daily activity and stay on their usual medication.

The other half did exactly the same, but they were also given 6-8 hours of weekly community service — nursing homes, children's hospitals, Meals-On-Wheels.

After six weeks, strength was re-evaluated. Without exception, all the community service members, the so-called "involved" group, had significant increases in muscle potency.

Involvement is good medicine.

The Love of Forgiving

The ultimate measure of involvement comes from the ability to say and *feel*, "I forgive you." The truly loving person understands that pure involvement is not restricted to those who love us in return. It includes those who have hurt us as well as those close to us.

Buried anger breeds resentment, which lowers immunity and resistance to illness. Stress causes heart disease, hypertension and maybe even cancer. Herbert Benson, Harvard cardiologist and author of *The Relaxation Response*, has documented this in a professional, convincing manner. Lack of ability to forgive first oneself and then others is self destructive, suicidal.

To live is to serve. To serve is to love. Albert Schweitzer said, "One thing I know: the only ones among you who will be really happy are those who will have sought and found how to serve."

Dedicating our lives to others allows love to come full circle. It permits the ultimate realization of who we are and the nature of our destiny.

I end this chapter with an inspirational verse found in Old St. Paul's Church in Baltimore, Maryland.

Desiderata

Go placidly amid the noise and haste, and remember what peace there is in silence. As far as possible without surrender be on good terms with all persons. Speak your truth quietly and clearly, listen to others, even the dull and ignorant. They, too, have their story. Avoid loud aggressive persons, they are vexations to the spirit. If you compare yourself with others, you may become vain and bitter, for always there will be greater and lesser persons than yourself. Enjoy your achievements as well as your plans. Keep interested in your career, however humble, it is a real possession in the changing fortunes of time. Exercise caution in your business affairs, for the world is full of trickery. But let this not blind you to what virtue there is, many people strive for high ideals. And everywhere life is full of heroism. Be yourself. Especially do not feign affection. Neither be cynical about love, for in the face of all aridity and disenchantment it is as perennial as the grass. Take kindly the council of the years, gracefully surrendering the things of youth. Nurture strength of spirit to shield you in sudden misfortune. But do not distress yourself with imaginings. Many fears are born of loneliness and fatigue. Beyond a wholesome discipline, be gentle with yourself. You are a child of the universe no less than the trees and the stars. You have a right to be here. And whether it is clear to you or not no doubt the universe is unfolding as it should. Therefore be at peace with God whatever you conceive him to be, and whatever your labors and aspirations in the noisy confusion of life, keep peace with your soul. With all its sham, drudgery and broken dreams, it is still a beautiful world. Be careful. Strive to be happy.

Anonymous
November, 1692

Wellsprings

Avoid fried meats which might angry up the blood. If your
stomach disputes you, lie down and pacify it with cool thoughts.
Keep the juices flowing by jaggling around gently as you move.
Go very light on the vices, such as carrying on in society.
The social ramble ain't restful. Avoid running at all times.
Don't look back. Something might be gaining on you.

Satchel Paige

Teach the Children

It is never too late to have a happy childhood.
Anonymous

Life, love and laughter —
what priceless gifts to give our children.
Phyllis Campbell Dryden

Because of the philosophy I espouse, I am invited to speak to a wide spectrum of audiences — Elks, Moose, Owls, Kiwanis (not sure what kind of animal that is) . . . Lutherans, Catholics, Unitarians, Jews, Baptists . . . Senior Citizens (they prefer "mature Americans"), young adults.

The audiences I hesitate with the most, even though my wife and I have raised two girls of our own, are youth groups or schools. My outspoken opinions on the power of attitude puts me in an uncomfort- able position at times.

Teens are not impressed by *The Attitude Thing*.

Going to a school full of soon-to-be adults to talk about how tragedy can teach, is a little like trying to sell fudge to the candy man. You have to be a pretty skilled salesman to be successful. For one thing, most adolescents fortunately have had little calamity enter their lives. For them, catastrophe is a broken date, a D+ in math, or the words *What party?*. Their souls have not been tempered with truly trying times. Maturity and growth wait just around the bend.

Interaction with an audience of teenagers often generates blank stares as though they had just received a healthy dose of novocaine. They gape vacantly, responding much as the numbed mouth does to the dentist's drill.

I try not to practice scare tactics, but gentle discussions about the transience of life and the need to live fully in the moment are often met with pubescent misunderstanding or confusion. Let's face it, kids think they will <u>never</u> die. They are invincible, indestructible . . . until a classmates winds up on an ICU ventilator after a car accident.

This is why I include a chapter on the exceptional person's need to leave behind a legacy of worth for the children.

> *A child learns by wiggling skills through his fingers*
> *and toes and into himself. By soaking up habits*
> *and attitudes of those around him. Day by day the*
> *child comes to know a little bit more about what*
> *you know, a little bit more about what you think, to*
> *understand your understanding. What you dream*
> *and believe becomes your children. Whether you*
> *perceive dully or clearly, whether you think fuzzily*
> *or sharply as you behave foolishly or wisely, as you*
> *dream drably or goldenly, as you bear false witness*
> *or tell the truth, thus your child learns.*
> Frederick Moffett, New York educator

Children often have poor or no role models. TV has become the mentor, pal, baby-sitter and pseudo-parent. The average pre-K child of five has watched 7,000+ hours of television before stepping foot into a classroom. Imagine Sesame Street, the Discovery and the Learning channels . . . but also hour after hour of MTV, HBO and violent, sex-filled movies. I am not on a soapbox demanding tighter control or stricter enforcement of the airwaves. I am concerned when preschool children are quizzed about "heroes" and names like Madonna and O.J. come up.

Attitudes learned in the preschool years remain imbedded throughout adulthood. So, we must provide positive, enriching role models for our children, instead of allowing elements of the media to become surrogate parents of questionable integrity.

Yes, yes, I know. I read like conservative, preachy bosh. But, it greatly concerns me that suicide, murder, sexual harassment and domestic violence are all on the rise. And I have a grand desire to leave the world a better place for our children.

Learning starts in infancy. Holding, touching, loving. From the moment of birth, even an infant knows if it is wanted. Newborns held and cuddled do much better than those ignored or held infrequently. It is impossible to show or say *I love you* too much to a child. There are many societal forces at work that go out of their way to inform them of the opposite. Let us tilt the scales back towards love that is enriching, secure and responsible.

Also remember, discipline and setting rules and boundaries are a vital part of loving our children.

———◆———

Gilda Radner's witty, touching book *It's Always Something*, bravely relates her battle with metastatic ovarian cancer and the learning process birthed by calamity. The book's last paragraph is its most poignant and endearing.

Given the opportunity to leave your epitaph, what would you write? About things you've seen, learned or felt? People whose lives you have touched? Well, Gilda talked about children:

When I was little, Dibby's cousin had a dog, just a mutt, and the dog was pregnant. I don't know how long dogs are pregnant, but she was due to have her puppies in about a week. She was out in the yard one day and got in the way of the lawn mower, and her two hind legs got cut off. They rushed her to the vet and he said, 'I can sew her up, or you can put her to sleep if you want, but the puppies are okay. She'll be able to deliver the puppies.'

Dibby's cousin said, 'Keep her alive.'

So the vet sewed up her back-side and over the next week the dog learned to walk. She didn't spend any time worrying, she just learned to walk by taking two steps in the front and flipping up her backside, then taking two steps and flipping up her backside again. She gave birth to six little puppies, all in perfect health. She nursed them and then weaned them. When they learned to walk, they all walked like her.

Every day of your life, you give yourself gifts — joy, sorrow, forgiveness, resentment, love and apathy. Because of imprinting and modeling, these are the same gifts which you simultaneously give to your children. We are all teachers yet do not appreciate the tremendous power we have to mold and shape.

To *teach* means to *lead out*, to *show the way*, and to *facilitate*. For some, the school of life, where we stand at the lectern, has become

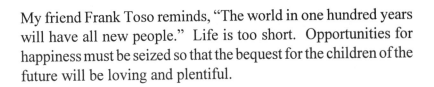

a joyless, mindless vacuum. If our teaching and mentoring style discourages happiness, creativity and growth, then we must alter our course and examine our values. We must make the conscious decision to love and show the way for those who follow.

It must begin with me. And you. Now.

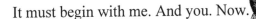

My friend Frank Toso reminds, "The world in one hundred years will have all new people." Life is too short. Opportunities for happiness must be seized so that the bequest for the children of the future will be loving and plentiful.

Songstress Whitney Huston expresses this sentiment:

> ### The Greatest Love of All
> *I believe that children are our future.*
> *Teach them well and let them lead the way.*
> *Show them all the beauty they possess inside.*
> *Give them a sense of pride.*
> *To make it easier let the children's laughter,*
> *remind us how we used to be.*

Play and laughter are part of life, but too often we have lost the child within. The needs of our inner child are ignored. In our support group sessions, we use a meditation, borrowed from self-help guru C. W. Metcalf. It helps us rediscover our lost child.

Relax. Breathe deeply and slowly through your nose and allow your eyes to close. . . . Go back to a time when you were four or five years old. . . . Life was an amazement, full of constant discovery and adventure. . . . In a safe place you create, filled with peace, light and life, notice the younger you, the child that was you at play. Encounter that child.

Look deeply into one another and touch each other's faces. Tell that child, now sitting upon your knee, how much life holds in store. Its pains and its joys.

Encourage that child to stay flexible, loose and ready to

counter sorrow with laughter and amazement. . . . Empower that child with the growth necessary to withstand the onslaught of growing up, its disappointments and bitter moments.

Finally, remember that child is always with you as you allow that little one to meld within you and become your heartbeat! The memory of that happy youngster is, in truth, always with you whenever you choose to permit it.

This meditation helps us realize that our young one has never left us and is always with us, a life companion urging us, if you will, to experience childlike wonder at the world, even as an adult.

Wordsworth said it so beautifully:
> *My heart leaps up when I behold*
> *A rainbow in the sky;*
> *So was it when my life began;*
> *So is it now I am a man;*
> *So be it when I shall grow old;*
> *Or let me die!*
> *The child is father of the man;*
> *And I could wish my days to be*
> *Bound each to each by natural piety.*

I know a man who carries in his wallet a creased black and white photo of a six-year old boy. When life gets him down, he gazes upon this yesteryear picture of himself. He remembers what is important — giggles, innocence and open-eyed wonder. His inner child's strength and resilience keep him soundly grounded.

————◆————

Teaching does not just impart knowledge of goodness, light, virtue and beauty. To be well rounded, we need to understand that confusion, loneliness and need are an integral part of growth and development.

My father has always been strong and resourceful. His fortitude and intellect held our family together during difficult times. Dad was also *real*, no story book character. But, only twice did I see my hero cry. Once, when he lost his job during my teens, then when my Uncle Sam died. Those episodes have stuck with me all these years not because they were so traumatic for me (They were!), but because they taught me that real people express feelings.

We all wish life could be happiness, beauty, joy and wonderment. But sorrow, regret, rejection, unhappiness, depression and gloom come, too. All teach volumes. Do not withhold these learning tools from the children or you will block them from wholeness. With you as a guide, teacher, role model, and support system, let your children experience and understand the good as well as the bad of life. Teach children that human beings are finely tuned miracles who thrive on what is good and wholesome.

———— • ————

Poet Robert Browning encouraged that "A man's reach should exceed his grasp, or what's a heaven for?"

Teach children not to settle for an average, okay, good-enough, middle-of-the-road life and not to be restricted by pigeon holes and labels. Instead, show them that aiming for the moon is not too high, even if you have to achieve amid kicking and screaming.

Mentoring's magical symbiosis is that giver and receiver have their investment interest compounded daily while harvesting life's richness. Experiencing a deep relationship with another teaches the possibilities of becoming fully human. This learning intimacy is the alternative to despair, loneliness . . . death.

R. D. Laing, in his *Politics of Experience*, says, "We think much less than we know. We know much less than what we love. We love much less than what there is. And to this precise extent we are much less than what we are."

Our fear of sharing and refusal to love our children through proper modeling may have dire consequences. It may even jeopardize our race's future. Do not worry that you are incapable, incorrect or foolish as a teacher. The important thing is to try. We are all teachers. We are all children. No matter how *old* or impressive others may appear, most of us never mature. We simply grow taller and older. So, on our eternal road to maturity, we must not hesitate to give the children a lift.

On the first day, first hour of medical school anatomy class at Temple University, Professor Bob Troyer says to 150 petrified recruits, "Half of what you'll learn in the next four years is wrong. Dead wrong. But the problem is none of us know which half! So, learn it all, understanding that medicine is not an exact science." . . . Just like life.

And understand too that children teach as well as learn. Realize that none of us is too old to rethink, to relearn, or to start over. Actor Billy Crystal, in the comedy *City Slickers*, consoles a friend by reminding him of the game *Start Over* that they played as children. It is a little like calling, "Olley, olley, oxen free!" after a game of Hide-and-Seek. It wipes the slate clean, allowing us to begin fresh. Children have taught me that it is all right to begin again, to forgive and start over, and to wipe our slate clean.

"Why?" is the eternal, ubiquitous, shoehorn question of childhood. Try to bluff a child. Fib, fake it, or dodge the query and see how quickly the youngster will let you off the hook.

If I am not confident, secure and centered, I cannot be the best teacher. Children teach courage by confronting all that can be imagined. Remember those one-way nursery school mirrors? I stopped to pick up our oldest daughter one day; and arriving early, I went into a waiting area containing a large window where parents could unobtrusively observe their little ones at play. My eyes, and soon my heart, watched Amy.

Children were grouped in various forms of play. There was my daughter — alone — with toy in hand. It did not take me long to figure out what was happening. Amy walked from group to group asking, "Will you play with me?" Each group denied her access. When she ran out of gatherings, she did not sit in a corner, take twenty Valium, and sleep for a week. She did not wail, "No one loves me!" and did not contemplate suicide. Instead, she went into a neutral area and amused herself with the toy. Pretty soon a little boy joined her.

I thought about this later and understood the valuable lesson I had observed. There are always viable alternatives to rejection, a myriad of other possibilities. One need only to seek and then choose. Even a child knows.

Finally we learn from children that *knowing* something but not *doing*, is really not knowing at all. *Talking* about ideas without active *involvement* is not being involved at all.

My youngest daughter, Karen, makes me very proud. This sensitive and giving child understands that doing must support rhetoric. She and a group of friends volunteer weekly at an AIDS hospice. She serves meals and spends quality time visiting with the residents. In so doing, she puts her words into action, giving wonderful example to those quick to condemn or rush away from those marked with this unfortunate, tragic ailment.

The verse "You will know them, not by their tongues, but by their actions" imparts Biblical wisdom.

Education is not just what is rotely taught in classrooms. Learning occurs when we are open to our own possibilities. The ability to both teach and to learn from children is one of the greatest possibilities of all.

Wellsprings

The hope for tomorrow lies in truth, youth and love.
R. Buckminster Fuller

Epilogue

Endings are only beginnings, backwards.

Neil Simon, *The Good-bye Girl*

I have a modest liquor cabinet at home. A bottle of presentable gin . . . a little Scotch for my dad . . . the obligatory makings of a Manhattan for my mother-in-law . . . and a row of Bailey's Irish Cream.

The Bailey's are milestones of sorts. For the past nine years, I have received this gift on St. Patrick's Day from two of my favorite leprechauns, Paul and Betty Long. Usually the bottle is accompanied by a button touting *Honorary Irishman.* Each bottle is a fitting celebration of another cancer-free year by Paul, one of two long-term, pancreatic cancer survivors I have been privileged to know and help heal.

Paul's winsome smile and easy way are outer wrappings for a fierce inner determination to survive. His stellar character embodies each of the characteristics addressed in this book. He is responsible for himself like no one else I know. He questions anything that needs clarification and seeks opinions from physicians he trusts. Choice, risk, spirituality, living in the moment — all are cornerstones in his life. He and

Betty, his personal support *group*, reach out through church activities that fill their lives with purpose and grace.

I mention this as I hunt for the scotch behind a citadel of Bailey's. Dad is coming over and I am certain he will ask for Johnnie Walker. I will drink a toast of Bailey's to my friends, the Longs. They have taught me the role of Healer.

Then there's Jim Jewell, a thoracic surgeon with a heart as big as they come. In the twenty years I have known him, he has been my touchstone, the one I silently observe when I want to know how to be a good physician. He started his career in medicine in tandem with his wife Eleanor, a nurse. Now at his career's end, he and Eleanor minister to the physical and spiritual needs of Africans.

His surgery skills are deeply appreciated. "There is so much to do. We make a little bit of difference, but the people are genuinely thankful for *anything* we give." He has spent over five years there in two separate stints, and the Jewells are contemplating a third tour of volunteer duty.

Thoreau's Walden Pond exhortation is to *simplify, simplify, simplify.* But most people seem to *complicate, complicate, complicate.* Jim and Eleanor have reduced their mission to one very simple precept. *Give all you can with all that you have.*

I am not cut out to go to Africa, nor am I asking you pack your bags. It takes people of extraordinary love and fullness of spirit to serve in this way. I do realize, however, that the pure physician is capable of such humanitarianism. Such a physician knows that with the gift of healing, all things are possible. Many lives can and must be touched.

———•———

It has been a great source of fun and satisfaction compiling interesting, inspiring stories for this book. Ten years ago I began speaking to small groups about the necessity for humanistic action within my profession. Over time, I have spoken to a wide range of interested audiences. Ironically, the one group that appears the least interested in what I have to say are doctors themselves.

It has been painful for me to ignore the labels. *Maverick. Renegade. Oddball.* But — slowly — the medical profession is turning around. For all the right reasons, the vast majority of physicians are hearing and listening to the demands of their charges. People demand excellent health care, holistic in approach. And we are beginning to comply.

The practice of medicine is more than a job or service. Medicine is a calling, a vocation. It demands training and dedication like few other fields. Even though its practitioners are held in high esteem, they have no right to demand blind faith of those they serve.

Medicine is a *practice* not a predictable science. Patients need to see their doctors as real human beings, capable of errors. In so doing, they will understand our humanness and shortcomings as well as feel a closer kinship and approachability.

But never should physicians stand aloof and apart from their patients. We are all cut from the same cloth by Our Creator.

Pain and suffering, joy and ecstasy, life and death, the humdrum of everyday living are experienced by all in the medical profession, too. We are not gods. We use the john, make mistakes, have shortcomings, and face our daily problems just like everyone else.

The good physician should be a resource, a beautifully turned touchstone capable of leading both himself and his patients to wholeness. He serves as a guide or an instrument, but never as the prime mover. All healing comes from Our Creator. We act as true physicians when we channel His healing power for the good of mankind.

I have spent many pages describing the characteristics of self healing and what must be done to achieve oneness of body and mind and completeness of person. But, I have offered little concrete activity to accomplish this end.

It is one thing to say laugh instead of languish, move forward instead of back, be positive instead of negative. Yet, how does one find humor in tragedy, resilience in travesty, reason in madness?

One truism I can offer is that _choice_ is vital to complete health. But how do we know what to choose in the face of the monster of malignancy? How do we keep from screaming in the night when the diagnosis of ALS or MS is laid upon us? To whom do we turn when the diagnosis is AIDS?

There are no life scripts. We cannot go to the library and find answers in the back of _The Book of Life_. Rather, the answers we seek are internally deep within where things can get dark and spooky. The experiences I have discussed in this book have solutions that perhaps will not work for you. But I offer these noble stories as a source of options for those in need of strength, resolution and answers.

Back to Billy Crystal as Mitch in _City Slickers_. He continually bugs the enigmatic Curley to tell "the secret to life." Finally, Curley appears primed to expound. He holds up his index finger. "Yes! What! What is it?" asks Mitch.

". . . that's for you to find out," Curley retorts.

And so I say to you, find out the meaning of your life. Figure out your _own_ best way to use the guidelines I have discussed. But, for God's sake, for your loved one's sake:

Fight!
Live!
Do something!

For _your own_ life's sake . . .

Wellsprings

"The lack of fear is not courage.
It is instead some kind of brain damage!"
    M. Scott Peck, *The Road Less Traveled*

Appendix

A call for help or information is very often one of the steps involved in the healing process. The following list is a compilation of national as well as Berks County, Pennsylvania resources.

If you need a resource that is not in this index, consult your telephone directory or contact:

•National Self-Help Clearinghouse
25 West 43rd Street, Room 620
New York, NY 10036
(212) 642-2944

AIDS

•AIDS Hotline   **(800) 342-2437**

• **Project Inform**   **(415) 558-8669**
  19655 Market Street, Suite 220
  San Francisco, CA 94103

• **Berks AIDS Network Hotline**   **(610) 375-2242**
  429 Walnut Street
  Reading, PA 19601

Alcohol Abuse

- **Alcoholics Anonymous (AA)**   (212) 870-3400
  General Service Office
  475 Riverside Drive
  New York, NY 10115

- **Al-Anon Family Headquarters**   (212) 302-7240
  200 Park Avenue South
  New York, NY 10003

- **Al-Anon Berks County**   (610) 373-5237

- **Caron Counseling Service**   (610) 373-5447
  845 North Park Road
  Wyomissing, PA 19610

- **National Council on Alcoholism**   (610) 372-8917
  and Drug Dependence of
  Berks County

Cancer

- **Cancer Information Service**   (800)4-CANCER

- **ECap**   (800) 700-8869
  (Exceptional Cancer Patients)   (203) 343-5950
  300 Plaza Middlesex
  Middletown, CT 06457

- **American Cancer Society**   (610) 921-2328
  Berks County Unit
  498 Bellevue Avenue
  Reading, PA 19601

Children's & Teens'
Crisis Intervention

- **Covenant House**   **(800) 999-9999**

- **Kid Save**   **(800) 543-7283**

- **National Committee for**   **(312) 663-3520**
  Prevention of Child Abuse
  322 South Michigan Avenue
  Chicago, IL 60604

- **Berks County Children**   **(610) 478-6700**
  and Youth Services

- **Children's Home of Reading**   **(610) 478-8266**
  1010 Centre Avenue
  Reading, PA 19601

- **Pro-Kids of Berks County Inc.**   **(610) 670-1670**
  2909 Windmill Road
  Sinking Spring, PA 19608

Drug Abuse

- **National Institute of**   **Info:**   **(301) 443-6245**
  Drug Abuse (NIDA)   **Help:**   **(800) 662-4357**
  Parklawn Building
  5600 Fishers Lane, Room IOA-39
  Rockville, MD 20852

- **Caron Counseling Services**   (see alcohol abuse)

- **Council on Chemical Abuse**   **(610) 378-6186**

- **Narcotics Anonymous**   **(610) 374-5944**

Women's Issues

- **Austin Rape Crisis Center**   **(512) 440-7273**
  1824 East Oltorf
  Austin, TX 78741

- **National Coalition**   **(800) 333-7233**
  Against Domestic Violence
  P.O. Box 34103
  Washington, DC 20043-4103

- **Berks Women in Crisis**   **(610) 372-9540**

- **Birthright of Berks County Inc.**   **(610) 374-8545**
  125 South 5th Avenue
  West Reading, PA 19611

Volunteer Services

- **American Red Cross**   (610) 375-4383
  Berks County Chapter

- **Berks County Office of Aging**   (610) 478-6500

- **Big Brothers/Big Sisters**   (610) 796-9919
  of Berks County

- **Junior League of Reading, PA Inc.**   (610) 320-4919

- **National Multiple Sclerosis Society**   (610) 376-6566

- **Police Athletic League**   (610) 376-7299
  of Greater Reading

- **Rainbow Home of Berks County**   (610) 678-6172

- **Volunteer Center of United Way**   (610) 371-4571
  of Berks County

Touchstones

When was the last time you wrote a thank you letter?

Suggested Readings

Benson, Herbert, with Miriam Z. Klipper. "The Relaxation Response." New York: Avon Books, 1976.

Berg, Elizabeth. "Talk Before Sleep." New York: Random House, 1994.

Borysenko, Joan. "Minding the Body, Mending the Mind." Reading, Mass.: Addison Wesley, 1987; New York: Bantam Books, 1988.

Buscaglia, Leo F., Ph.D. "Living, Loving & Learning." New York: Ballantine Books, 1982.

Campbell, Joseph. "The Hero With a Thousand Faces." Princeton: Princeton University Press, 1968.

Campbell, Joseph, with Bill Moyers. "The Power of Myth." New York: Double Day, 1988.

Canfield, Jack and Mark Victor Hansen. "Chicken Soup for the Soul." Deerfield Beach, Fl.: Health Communications, 1993.

Canfield, Jack and Mark Victor Hansen. "A Second Helping of Chicken Soup for the Soul." Deerfield Beach, Fl.: Health Communications, 1994.

Cousins, Norman. "Anatomy of an Illness as Perceived by the Patient." New York: Norton, 1979; New York: Bantam, 1981.

Frankl, Viktor. "Man's Search for Meaning." New York: Touchstone, 1984.

Fulghum, Robert. "All I Really Needed to Know I Learned in Kindergarten." New York: Villard Books, 1989.

Hammerskjöld, D. "Markings." New York: Alfred A. Knopf, 1964.

Jampolsky, Gerald. "Love is Letting Go of Fear." Millbrae, Calif.: Celestial Arts, 1979.

Kübler-Ross, Elisabeth. "On Death and Dying." New York: Macmillan, 1969.

Kübler-Ross, Elisabeth. "Death: The Final Stage of Growth." Englewood Cliffs, N.J.: Prentice-Hall, 1975.

Kübler-Ross, Elisabeth. "To Live Until We Say Goodbye." Englewood Cliffs, N.J.: Prentice-Hall, 1978.

Kushner, Harold S. "When Bad Things Happen to Good People." New York: Schocken, 1981; New York: Avon, 1983.

Laing R.D. "The Politics of Experience." New York: Ballantine Books, 1976.

McCurley, Foster and Alan Weitzman. "Making Sense Out of Sorrow." Valley Forge, Pa: Trinity Press International, 1995.

Moody, Raymond A., Jr. "Life After Life." Covington, Ga.: Mockingbird Books, 1975; New York: Bantam, 1976.

Peck, M. Scott, M.D. "Further Along the Road Less Traveled." New York: Simon & Schuster, 1993.

Radner, Gilda. "It's Always Something." New York: Simon & Schuster, 1989.

Schueman, Helen A. "A Course in Miracles." Tiburon, Calif.: Foundation for Inner Peace, 1976.

Siegel, Bernie S., M.D. "How to Live Between Office Visits." New York: Harper Collins, 1993.

Siegel, Bernie S., M.D. "Love, Medicine & Miracles." New York: Harper & Row, 1986.

Siegel, Bernie S., M.D. "Peace, Love & Healing." New York: Harper & Row, 1989.

Simonton, 0. Carl, Stephanie Matthews-Simonton and James Creighton. "Getting Well Again." Los Angeles: J.P. Tarcher, 1978; New York: Bantam Books, 1980.

Solzhenitsyn, Aleksandr. "Cancer Ward." Translated by Nicholas Bethell and David Burg. New York: Farrar, Straus & Giroux, 1969; New York: Bantam Books, 1969.

St. Exupéry A. de. "The Little Prince." New York: Harcourt Brace Jovanovitch, 1971.

Taylor, John A. "Notes on an Unhurried Journey." New York: Four Walls Eight Windows, 1991.

Topf, Linda Noble, M.A., with Hal Zena Bennett, Ph.D. "You Are Not Your Illness." New York: Simon & Schuster, 1995.

Wellsprings

Do all the good you can,
By all the means you can,
In all the ways you can,
At all the times you can,
To all the people you can,
As long as ever you can.

John Wesley's Rule

About the Author

Photograph by Gretchen Hardy

Dr. Leo Frangipane grew up in South Philly amid the smells of pasta and the music of Bandstand. The love of his Italian family and the drive to "be somebody" guided him through Temple University Medical School and a residency and fellowship in surgery at The Hospital of the University of Pennsylvania. He then established a highly successful surgical practice in Berks County. Along the way, he lost two things — his hair (as he will affably point out with a booming laugh) and assurance that his life had deeper meaning.

Of course, we have all grappled with that age-old quest for meaning, but Dr. Frangipane did something profound. He went on a quest where his spirituality and his patients were the center of his being. He left his group practice and, although terrified, set up a private practice that could have been painted by Norman Rockwell.

He hugged. He wept. He told jokes. He sang Italian arias during surgery. He listened and spent time getting to know the person, not "the gall bladder" or "the mastectomy." Every day he stood by his patients as they faced horrible diseases, tough decisions, fear, anger, and sometimes even death.

His spirituality gave him strength, joy and a deep sense of meaning. He heard a resounding message from his patients: *Life is a trip, not a goal.* Dr. Frangipane is very active in support groups for those suffering disabling and terminal illnesses. He navigates with families through their difficult times. His message of joy and love, determination and hope, strength and nobility has been heard by thousands in audiences along the east coast and other major cities.

Dr. Frangipane lives with his wife, Joyce, and their daughters, Amy and Karen, outside Reading, Pennsylvania.

Every so often someone comes along whose
message we hear with our hearts.
    ... who beats to our drummer.
    ... who plays our song.

Spreading the Word

Perhaps you are in the middle of planning program speakers for the upcoming year. Last year your organization may have heard all about the struggles of weight loss, the duplicity of politics, and the changes in healthcare. This year you want to bring in speakers who will enrich the lives of your members, put lanolin on their stresses, and a chuckle over care lines. You want a speaker who will draw deeply into hearts and minds and send you home with a message that is relevant and uplifting.

Now that you have read Dr. Frangipane's book, you know this unique man has a very special message to deliver.

If you are part of an organization that would be helped by living joyfully today and not regretting yesterday or fearing tomorrow, if your lives need to be reconnected with a deeper meaning, if you want to laugh and, yes, even shed a tear, then call or write to schedule Dr. Frangipane's talk, *Touchstones & Wellsprings*.

Don't miss this unique, enriching opportunity.

Leo G. Frangipane, Jr., M.D.
P.O. Box 6923
Wyomissing, PA 19610

(610) 375-6000

 Wellsprings

Things may come to those who wait.
But only the things left by those who hustle.

Abraham Lincoln

Ordering by Mail

We would be happy to ship Dr. Frangipane's
message to you, a friend, or loved one.

Book	**$11.00**
Tape Cassette	**$11.00**
VHS Video	**$15.00**

<u>Call</u>:   or   **Mail coupon below to:**
(610) 375-6000   **Leo G. Frangipane, Jr., M.D.**
                              P.O. Box 6923
                              Wyomissing, PA 19610

Please send the following copies of

Touchstones and Wellsprings

Paperback Book	___ copies at $11.00 each	Total	$_____
Tape Cassette	___ copies at $11.00 each	Total	$_____
VHS Video	___ copies at $15.00 each	Total	$_____
		Subtotal	$_____
	(PA residents add 6% sales tax)		$_____
	S/H: add $2 for <u>each item</u> ordered		$_____
		Total	$_____

Send to me:
Name _____
Phone (_____) _____
Address _____
City _____ State ____ Zip _____
          Send: _____ Book _____ Cassette _____ Video

Also send in my name to:
Name _____
Address _____
City _____ State ____ Zip _____
          Send: _____ Book _____ Cassette _____ Video

Photocopy order sheet if you would like us to send to others.
2 weeks delivery. Make checks payable to Leo G. Frangipane, Jr., M.D.

Dialogue

Gentle Friend,
Your love and support is very special. I value
any words you share about **Touchstones and Wellsprings**.
God bless and keep you!

Dr. Leo

_____
_____
_____
_____
_____
_____
_____
_____
_____
_____
_____
_____

Ordering by Mail

We would be happy to ship Dr. Frangipane's message to you, a friend, or loved one.

Book	**$11.00**
Tape Cassette	**$11.00**
VHS Video	**$15.00**

Call: or   **Mail coupon below to:**
(610) 375-6000   **Leo G. Frangipane, Jr., M.D.**
P.O. Box 6923
Wyomissing, PA 19610

Please send the following copies of

Touchstones and Wellsprings

Paperback Book	___ copies at $11.00 each	Total	$_____
Tape Cassette	___ copies at $11.00 each	Total	$_____
VHS Video	___ copies at $15.00 each	Total	$_____
		Subtotal	$_____
	(PA residents add 6% sales tax)		$_____
	S/H: add $2 for each item ordered		$_____
		Total	$_____

Send to me:

Name _____

Phone (_____) _____

Address _____

City _____ State _____ Zip _____

Send: _____ Book _____ Cassette _____ Video

Also send in my name to:

Name _____

Address _____

City _____ State _____ Zip _____

Send: _____ Book _____ Cassette _____ Video

Photocopy order sheet if you would like us to send to others.
2 weeks delivery. Make checks payable to Leo G. Frangipane, Jr., M.D.

Dialogue

Gentle Friend,
Your love and support is very special. I value
any words you share about **Touchstones and Wellsprings**.
God bless and keep you!

Dr. Leo